Struggles to Love

Other titles by Kathy Galloway:

Imaging the Gospels (SPCK 1987)
Love Burning Deep (SPCK 1993)

STRUGGLES TO LOVE
The Spirituality of the Beatitudes

*

Kathy Galloway

First published in Great Britain 1994
Society for Promoting Christian Knowledge
Holy Trinity Church
Marylebone Road
London NW1 4DU

British Library Cataloguing-in-Publication Data
A catalogue record for this book is available from the British Library

ISBN 0-281-04740-5

Typeset by Action Typesetting Limited, Gloucester
Printed in Great Britain by
BPC Paperbacks Ltd

'We Alone' by Alice Walker, published in *Horses Make a Landscape
Look More Beautiful* (Women's Press, 1985), reprinted by permission of
the publisher.

Extracts from *Schindler's Ark* by Thomas Keneally (Hodder and
Stoughton Limited 1982), reprinted by permission of the publisher.

'Bill of Rights for Women' by the Scottish Women's Aid (Scottish
Women's Aid, 97 Morrison St, Edinburgh; unpublished), reprinted with
permission of the organisation.

Scriptural quotations taken from the *Good News Bible* (*Today's English
Version*) published by the Bible Societies and Collins, © American Bible
Society 1976. Reprinted with permission of the publisher.

Extracts from the *Authorised Version* (King James Version), the rights in
which are vested in the Crown in perpetuity within the United
Kingdom, are reproduced by permission of the Crown's patentee
Cambridge University Press.

For my children,
David, Duncan, and Helen Galloway,
for whose sake
it seems most important
to struggle to love.

CONTENTS

Acknowledgements

Any book is written by many people, though one person may find the words for it, and this book more than most. It has been shaped, as its author has, by a web of relationship that extends in many directions of time and place. I wish to acknowledge some of these, and to let those whom I thank by name represent the many I cannot name, but nevertheless are woven into the web of this book and this life.

My grateful thanks to those with whom I have sought, and often found common ground: in my first community of my family; in my first community of the church, St John's, Oxgangs, Edinburgh; in house churches in Govan and Partick, Glasgow; in the Stair Community in West Pilton, Edinburgh; in the Steering Committee of Scottish Churches Action for World Development; and most of all, in the Iona Community, in Iona and Glasgow. All of these have enabled me to feel 'God-encompassed, even in strange territory.'

Thanks also to those who have encouraged me in the writing of this book, and in my other writing; especially to Colin Gray, who refuses to allow me to get stuck in my deficiencies, and so assists me to extend what I can do; and to Philip Law, my editor at SPCK, who has had the sensitivity to allow this labour of love time to gestate and come to term.

We are not alone in our struggles to love (though sometimes it may feel that way). There are many whose friendship I value more than I can express, but I want to thank particularly Val Holtom, Penny Stuart and John

Acknowledgements

and Molly Harvey, who have accompanied me in tears and laughter, in words and silence, through some of my struggles to love.

Finally, I wish to thank those people whose stories I have told in this book. I hope they will forgive whatever shortcomings they find in them; any such do not stem from any lack of respect, and I have told their stories because I loved them. They, more than any preacher, academic, or expert, have been my profound theological influences. Because of them, and many like them, I have trusted enough to walk the road, even where the maps did not go.

Kathy Galloway
Glasgow, September 1993

Real

I'm not a symbol
I'm not a statistic
I'm not the inches in somebody's column.

I'm not admirable, but
I'm not pitiable either.
I'm simply human.

If you turned me inside out,
you'd find fury, fear, regret and sorrow
struggling with the love and the longing,
hope and wonder,
and all my neediness.

Please take these things seriously.
Don't pietize or glamorize or trivialize or sermonize.
They are the marks of my life,
gift and loss,
wound and offence.
Please respect them.

I am at odds with all that requires me to be a
    symbol.
I insist on being real.

STRUGGLES TO LOVE

The Spirituality of the Beatitudes

I was travelling on a train recently; I wasn't looking for conversation. I wanted to spend an hour or two reading peacefully—solitary journeys being one of the luxuries of a parent of three children. The train was busy and I sat down opposite a middle-aged, smartly dressed, rather tired-looking woman and got out my book. A few minutes later, a steward came along with coffee, and we both bought some. The woman started to make polite conversation, and I realized that she was eager to talk. Not without some reluctance, I put down my book. We talked about Christmas shopping, the unreliability of British Rail, the dreadful summer weather, and the splendours of Marks and Spencers—the kind of things that strangers talk about on trains. Then she began to talk about her regular trips to Scotland, where she had been brought up, from Barrow-in-Furness, where she had lived since her marriage twenty-five years before: trips to see an ageing father-in-law living alone and, more recently, to visit a brother-in-law with cancer.

Like many people, she had been frightened by this new fear striking within her family circle: frightened by the sight of a big, strong man in his forties with the flesh falling away, his hair falling out from the radiotherapy; frightened by the reminders of her own mortality. But she came anyway, every other weekend (her husband came on alternate weekends), and brought

1

chocolates and talked cheerfully to her brother-in-law about the future.

She talked to me about her family: her husband, who was a travelling salesman; her two daughters aged twenty-one and nineteen, one working as a secretary and the other at university in Salford. Then she talked about herself.

She worked as a waitress in a factory canteen, part-time work, and hard on the feet. But she didn't enjoy it, didn't get any satisfaction from it. She said she wanted to do something that was useful, and had wondered about auxiliary nursing with mentally handicapped children. 'You know,' she said, 'when your children grow up, the meaning goes out of your life. You want to do something that makes your life worth while, something that means something. When the girls were young I had that, but now I feel I'm just wasting my life, and it doesn't mean anything.'

A few minutes later, the train pulled into the station and we parted on the platform, wishing each other well.

I didn't think that her life was meaningless. I saw that she had raised a family caringly. She was, at some cost in time and money, supporting and encouraging one seriously ill relative and another elderly and lonely relative, not even of her own kin. She held down a dull job, was a faithful wife. Yet she wanted more, sought a greater meaning for her life. She had something very precious. She had the yearning. She was struggling to love.

The Latin-American Jesuit theologian Jon Sobrino defines 'spirituality' as 'profound motivation'. By this, he means those instincts, intuitions, longings, and desires—both of nature and of culture—that move us, inspire us (literally, 'breathe through us'), and shape, inform and fill our decisions and actions.

I find this a very helpful definition. First, it recognizes

that everyone has a spirituality, just as everyone has a physicality, and takes the word back from the clutches of piosity and a certain kind of religious imperialism.

Second, it avoids the damaging split that separates spirituality from materiality, sees them as in essence different and grades them into higher and lower categories, since our profound motivations always include physical, bodily needs and desires, whether we are conscious of it or not.

Third, it allows us to deal with reality, which is much more about what people do than about what they say. Profound motivation always shows up in how we act, and may differ from the way we say we intend to act (a fact painfully learned by pollsters at General Elections).

And finally, it is a definition that is value-free, properly so in my opinion. It is simply not helpful to sound off about the need for the recovery of spirituality, or more spirituality. This has a built-in value judgement that begs many questions. Our spirituality, our profound motivations are experienced subjectively; often they have their genesis in instincts and events over which we have little control and for which we can hardly be held responsible. A child who has experienced early physical or emotional abuse, for example, cannot be held responsible for being profoundly motivated by fear, and we have no right to make judgements on that motivation. (*Jesus* never did.) The proper area for value addition lies elsewhere. It is the difficult interface between intentions and actions, in the making actual of motivation at the point at which content in-forms and takes shape—where the spirit is given flesh.

And what adds value, what gives choices and decisions and actions their significance, are our ultimate concerns, our greatest good, that which is God for us—whether that ultimate concern is self, truth, knowledge, the people, power, profit, God as understood in religion, or the rejection of God.

It is the nature of our ultimate concern, our greatest good, that gives shape and form to our spirituality, our profound motivations,* that provide the framework for our value judgements. And it is at this interface between motivation and concern, in this place of tension and conflict and struggle, that choices are made and action occurs.

The Beatitudes are all about this interface, this meeting place, this struggle. The word 'beatitude' simply means blessing. 'Blessing' comes from two sources, from the Latin word *benedicere*, to speak well of, and from the word 'bliss', meaning gladness. So one might say that 'blessing' is a good word whose gift implies gladness in the one who receives. And to be blessed suggests receiving a gift that results in gladness or happiness—but not a light or frivolous kind of gladness, for the word also has connotations of something special (literally, of being consecrated, of being marked with blood). We might say it suggests a bitter-sweet happiness.

Jesus, speaking to his disciples, said that there were some people who knew this bitter-sweet happiness, this painful gladness. He didn't say it as if describing a law, a rule ('you ought to be like this and you'll get a gold star'). Rather, he pointed out blessedness where it already existed, recognized it, named it, saluted it, affirmed it. He said of those people, 'they are in the right place'.

Which of course to his hearers, and to many who have heard the Beatitudes since, did not make a lot of sense. By worldly standards (and I don't think they're much different now than they were then), happiness, blessedness, was something else. To be poor in spirit, to be sorrowful, to be humble, to hunger and thirst, to be merciful, pure in heart, peacemaking, *persecuted*, for God's sake—what has that got to do with blessing, with happiness? These are considered to be marks of failure,

4

dissent, subversion. They are words of hardship. They are words of struggle.

But if Jesus saw that these qualities of blessedness were 'in the right place', then he was saying that they revealed aspects, facets, of God-life, of God-likeness. Those who revealed them were therefore in solidarity with God. And their struggle was also in solidarity with God.

Each of these qualities or characteristics of blessedness implies and suggests its opposite—poverty implies the possibility of wealth, sorrow of joy, humility of pride, hunger and thirst for justice of injustice, mercy of indifference, purity of heart of the stagnant heart, peacemaking of hostility, persecution of safety. And there is always the temptation in us to settle for the easy way. But the blessed ones were the ones who, accepting the potential for the easy way within them, still engaged in the struggle to draw out of themselves what was also potential within them—God-likeness. They sought fullness of life, the growth of the other side of themselves, the integration of their motivations and their intentions, their spirituality, and their faith. They laid their lives on the line. This blessedness was forged in the fire not of the Church, but of the world, shaped by the experience of life, not withdrawal.

In the Beatitudes we are shown both the hungers, lacks, hurts, and hopes that motivated the blessed ones, and the concern that directed their drive, the Word that spoke to their spirit. And something of the nature of God-life, of the life of the Kingdom, is revealed to us.

And, as Jesus did, so I think it is true that we today see beatitude, blessedness, above all in the ordinary lives of ordinary people. Jesus lived with and addressed ordinary people, not the pious ones, the ones sure of their own self-righteousness. He talked in the language of everyday experience, rooted the good news firmly in the ground of the commonplace, because that was where blessedness was to be found—in the struggles to be whole, in the yearning to heal the separation of life, within and without, in the struggles to love. And his good news was that God affirmed these struggles—with all their achievements and their failures—with unconditional love. Judgement lies not in our weakness, failure, and shame, but in the refusal to engage as we are able. And the judgement is what we do to ourselves, in the wholeness we refuse, the fullness of life we turn our backs on. 'It was not to judge us, but to save us . . .'

The struggle, of whether and what and *how* to love, is deeply seen in the lives of people. Mostly, we just have to open our eyes to those around us—not perfect, often not good, often not in the Church—who have somehow stumbled on to the way that is the Way. In this book, I have tried to share some pictures of people in whom *I* have seen blessedness, and to invite you too to see such people around *you*.

1

THE GLORY IN THE GREY

Blessed Are the Poor in Spirit:
The Kingdom of Heaven Belongs to Them

❧❧ · ❧❧

'In 1976, I attempted suicide. This was an outward manifestation of an ongoing struggle against despair and feelings of hopelessness which threatened to overwhelm me.' These are the words with which Joyce began to tell her story in an article written for *Coracle*, the magazine of the Iona Community. They are profoundly pain-filled words—not at all what we would associate with sharing in the Kingdom of heaven. And yet they are part of a journey that has, and continues to encompass, both emptiness and fullness, both need and sufficiency.

The external circumstances of Joyce's life, though they lack the absolute material poverty of many in the world and of a growing number in this country, certainly do not suggest wealth, success, or status. She is divorced, the mother of two teenage sons, living on income support and maintenance in a council flat in one of Edinburgh's less desirable neighbourhoods. But I think she would not in any way see her life as impoverished in a material sense. More than almost anyone I know, she has the ability to create delight in the midst of drabness, to discover 'the glory in the grey'.

So how can it be possible to travel from the despair of a suicide attempt to living a life that is immensely creative, hopeful for other people, and commanding of respect? In telling her own story, she spoke at some length of her own pain, and of her discovery, along with Kahlil Gibran, the author of *The Prophet*, that the deeper that pain carves into your being, the more joy you can contain. And that is clearly demonstrated in her life, in both its positive and negative elements. Possessed of an artistic temperament, she has a temper to match. Often she experiences her life as being a bit like clawing her way up a steep hill, hanging on with bloody nails. But she reveals the glory and pity of life in the prisoners she paints, and finds jewelled style in the treasure-house of countless Oxfam shops, and splendour overflowing into the heart that she holds agonizingly open, ready to be filled with the Kingdom of heaven.

Her style is the first thing you notice about her. Slim and quick in her movements, she has long silver-blonde hair, sometimes piled high, sometimes loose around her shoulders. Her eyes are fringed with black, and pale skin contrasts with vivid pink lipstick. She smiles a lot, and has the laugh of a raucous angel, gurgling up from somewhere very deep within her. She has a wonderful voice, whose strong Scottish accent suggests her Midlothian roots in its inflections and phrases. She dresses strikingly, mostly in black, but it's not funereal or sober black. It's the black of beads and sequins and net and feathers, it is relieved by flashes of white lace petticoat, or pink or purple shirts, or the floating scarves she winds round her hair or her neck or her waist. And jewellery, lots of it: rings and bracelets and glittering earrings. Her physical presence is strong, dramatic, and uniquely beautiful.

She hasn't always looked that way. When I first knew her, her hair was short and neat, and she wore Laura Ashley dresses in pastel colours. But it is as if the sculpting of her inner life to reveal a truer, more adventurous self, finds one expression in her appearance. Whatever the reason, in disregarding fashion, she creates her own fashion, a fashion that is never out of fashion. And she does so on very little money. She says, 'I have made a "profession" of second-hand shopping. Ability to buy beautiful things does not depend on having a lot of money. Second-hand shopping is full of surprises, and protects me from the dismaying effects of too much choice in the big department stores. And because I rarely spend more than £4 to £5 on an item of clothing or household goods, it is painless to recycle these goods back into the charity shops, or to give them to friends.'

And, as you would expect, her house is the same—full of beautiful things and old furniture that wouldn't raise more than a few pounds in an auction, but, in her hands, take their place in creating an environment of distinctiveness. The most valuable items in the house are probably her paintings, drawings and sketches, which adorn all the walls—along with the artistic creations of her children. In her thirties, with two young children, Joyce followed a dream and went to art college. Since then, she has begun to gain increasing recognition as a portrait artist.

For several years she visited the home of George MacLeod, the founder of the Iona Community, and he sat for her in a relationship that was not always easy, but that resulted in the completion of a number of fine drawings of him prior to his death. Two of these were accepted by the National Portrait Gallery of Scotland. She also draws some of the prisoners in Saughton Prison, where she teaches German. These too are relationships of exchange—the gift of mutual vulnerability that is only possible where one's own brokenness is accepted and shared.

The immense creativity of Joyce's life—her children, her art, her loving relationships with people on the margins of society, her ability to make and discover beauty and humour in the most unlikely ways and places—has its cost, however. Her life is full of the paradoxes of the poor in spirit, yet who experience that the Kingdom of heaven belongs to them. In telling her own story, she wrote of her suicide attempt, 'I had not yet learned the value of containing pain, and my desperate bids to rid myself of it were at great cost to myself, and often to those I love. Now I am learning, in tiny stages, to respond creatively to my pain, to contain it, to see it as a gift . . .'

What I have seen in Joyce's life is only a particularly vivid and beautiful demonstration of what I see too in the lives of those many others who also make the choice to respond creatively to the pain and hurt of their lives and experience.

I see her learning to contain her own pain; not denying it or pretending it doesn't hurt or keeping a stiff upper lip; not locking it away in a hidden place where it can fester and poison and smoulder into resentful combustion; but not simply aiming it like a missile at the nearest target, dumping it on the handiest available receptacle. This containment is a holding, a bearing, a carrying. It is a letting pain be pain. It is the exact meaning of the word 'passion', allowing or suffering experience. It is not virtuous or noble or pious. It hurts like hell. It includes a spectrum of experience that runs all the way from ignominy and humiliation through fear, anxiety, physical and mental anguish, to anger, outrage, and a burning sense of injustice.

And yet I see also that this containment, this passion, is the seedbed, the very ground of creativity, of new life. Between the temptation to punish oneself with guilt and self-loathing, or to punish others with hostility and self-justification, lies the place of struggle, the urge to create new forms for holding the meaning and value of our experience. Another way of saying that might be to suggest that if we can contain pain between accepting forgiveness for ourselves and offering it to others, the energy and spirit released by letting go of our attempts to get rid of pain (and very demanding of energy they are) becomes energy and spirit for creativity and for new life.

This is a lifetime's learning. As Joyce says, it happens in tiny stages.

And I see her learning to welcome the emptiness, the gaps, the incompleteness in her life. If we do not recognize, or will not name, the hunger, the yearning, the desire for that which goes beyond our experience, we will not be open to be captivated by the new, to be surprised by joy. The hunger for love, the yearning for right relationships, the desire for beauty, are all needs that are not capable of being fulfilled by money, status, or success. These things may give us an adrenalin 'high' (as may many other equally destructive addictions), but their effect is fleeting and ultimately unsatisfying. The deeper longings cannot be achieved; they are only received in the grace of creation and creativity, in the grace of discipleship and struggle for justice, in the grace of community and solitude, in the grace of human love. That is to say, in the grace of God. So I perceive a kind of restlessness in the lives of the poor in spirit, a longing for the 'beyond in the midst', which is a precondition of receptiveness to grace, and very far from any kind of passive acquiescence in emptiness. We simultaneously hold our unfulfilment both as pain and possibility.

This too is a lifetime's learning.

And I see Joyce learning to love and value herself, not just her own achievements and delights, not even just her courage in struggle (because what appears as courage in the eyes of others mostly just feels like hanging on by the tips of our fingers to us), but the whole unique and irreplaceable and infuriating and tragic and funny human being that she is and ever more becomes. Sometimes this is the most difficult learning of all. 'We hurt, and suffer hell and hate ourselves' ... or we hurt other people, sometimes without meaning to. And some people have simply never had the experience of being unconditionally loved (or think they haven't) without which it's harder to trust. But there's a movement of emptiness, of becoming poor here, as well. Letting go of an ideal image of ourselves or others. Accepting our frailties as well as our strengths, and recognizing that they come from the same human stuff—indeed, what we struggle with or are shamed most by in ourselves may be exactly what someone else most values in us. And sometimes, letting go of a prideful bad image of ourselves too. It really *isn't* the case that everyone else in the whole world is precious and valuable—except us; that no one else is quite as loathsome as we are, that there's hope for everyone—except me. There's a certain comfort in hanging on to our guilt, our sinfulness, because it means we can avoid the challenge of change, and the pain of growth. And just being ordinary, being rather like everyone else, can be an experience of emptiness, especially if we tend to relish being the centre of attention.

I don't want to paint Joyce as a saint. She's far from being that, and I imagine that at times she could be very difficult to live with. Some people don't like her, and it is true that her flamboyance, her uninhibitedness, and her refusal to be bound by convention could be overpowering—and perhaps a little threatening—to more gentle souls. Nor has she healed all her wounds, resolved all her conflicts, transformed all her pain. A few months ago I was working on some poetry, attempting to hear different accents, tones, rhythms of speech; and I heard Joyce's voice clearly in my mind, so I wrote a poem trying to express it in her speech patterns. But the content was all mine, and vaguely related to some thoughts I was having about a play. The next time we met, I told her about this, and she asked to read the poem. I read it

to her while sitting outdoors on a hill in the sunshine.
This is it:

It's felt like clawing your way up a mountain.
Ken whit I mean?
One moment you're up there, just going along,
doing quite nicely, not great, but nothing much wrong.
All of a sudden, you're sliding doon on yer arse,
bumping into every damn rock on the way,
and you land up right at the bottom
a'bruised and battered, and no knowing
where the hell you are.

And you lie there for a long time.
You don't have the strength to move.
You dinnae ken whit way to go
or why you should bother.
And ye think 'how did I get here?
Did I jump or was I pushed?'

In the end, you just get fed up lyin' there.
You start to crawl.
A wee bit at a time.
No really knowin' where you're goin.
No lookin' back in case ye fa' again.
Maist o' the time, ye're hangin' on by yer fingernails,
and they're bloody.
And ye crawl, and then ye stop
and then ye crawl again.
And an awfy lot o' times ye slip back.

But then ye notice that ye've actually
come quite a lang way.
Ye get sair knees, though.
And ye lose yer nerve a lot.
Get stuck half-way up a mountain
hangin' on for dear life.
Just like now.

When I finished reading it, she wept for a long time.

No, it's not so much healing, in the sense of mending, as a willingness to make the broken places sing.

In celebrating her own abundance, Joyce says, 'There are still times when I feel worn down by grinding poverty and by the grey streets where I live. But my ability to discover glory in the grey increases in proportion to growth of inner resources.' I don't know if she knows this, but, to many, she herself is glory in the grey.

SILVER

I remember the most valuable gift I ever received. I had been shopping in Princes Street in the centre of Edinburgh with my eldest son, who was then a toddler. It was one of Edinburgh's famous east-windy days, and David was warmly wrapped up in a furry red suit and tucked cosily into his buggy, with little visible apart from his glowing scarlet cheeks and his bright blue eyes. We were standing on a corner at the West End of Princes Street, waiting to meet a friend, when a tramp wandered up to us and engaged us in conversation. Perhaps he stopped to talk because he too had a pram!

He was the genuine article, not just someone down on his luck or, since it was a dozen years ago, one of the growing army of homeless young people. This was a dosser, a down-and-out: matted grey hair and beard, layers of filthy clothing topped by a disreputable greatcoat tied with a piece of rope, and shabby boots. The ancient pram seemed to be (probably was) filled with junk, covered with layers of newspaper. It looked as if it could quite easily move off on its own. There was a smell. But he was being quite sociable, not at all threatening. So we talked for a few minutes about Edinburgh's terrible weather. Then he turned his attention to my son David, who, being a small child, was quite undiscriminating in his affection. He beamed and gurgled at this strange man stooping to tickle him under the chin.

I saw my friend coming along the road, and made as if to move off. 'Wait, wait,' said the tramp. I wasn't sure what he meant, but I waited for a minute. He began to rummage around in the pockets of his greatcoat, came out empty-handed, and dived under the coat into another deeper pocket. Finally, triumphantly, he came out with something clasped in his hand. He bent down and put it into David's hand. He smiled at David, and David smiled at him. Then he bid us farewell, and wandered off. I opened David's closed fist and discovered that it held a ten-pence piece. My child, fed, housed, warm, healthy, and loved, had been given silver by a tramp.

I have never, before or since, received such generosity. I have never been given all that someone had to give. It is one of the great blessings of my life.

❦ · ❦

GOD-ENCOMPASSED
EVEN IN STRANGE TERRITORY

There are a lot of ways of being over-full, of having no room to receive. There's an old saying in Scotland: 'him! . . . I kent [knew] his faither!' It's the Scottish way of demonstrating that a prophet is without honour in his own land. Remember how Jesus had returned to Nazareth, his home town, had gone into the synagogue, had read the proclamation from the book of the prophet Isaiah, and then, in a truly stupendous claim, had identified himself as being the one to whom the prophecy referred. Remember the reaction of the townspeople. Imagine the scene! Local boy goes away and becomes well known in surrounding places. He comes into church and impresses everyone with how well he reads the Scriptures, and how

15

eloquently he speaks. The Gospel says that they were well impressed. You can just hear them whispering to each other: 'Isn't that Joseph's boy?'; you can just feel the glow of regional pride—here's one of our own, making good, doing well for himself.

But Jesus didn't bow his head modestly and accept their compliments. He didn't say, 'Yes, and I owe it all to my home town which made me what I am today.' Quite the contrary. He actually went on the attack, suggesting that it will not be long before 'Isn't that Joseph's boy?' becomes 'Oh, it's only Joseph's boy.' He suggested that it wouldn't be long before they started muttering, 'Why don't you solve your own problems before you start lecturing us about ours.' He suggests that soon they'll be challenging him to perform the same miracles in Nazareth that he had performed in Capernaum. And finally, to add insult to injury, he reminded them of several events in Jewish history when the people who thought they were special, that they could bask in reflected glory, were passed over in favour of foreigners. It was all a real slap in the face from the local boy made good.

And when the people heard it, they changed their tune very quickly. Their approval was surface in the extreme. And they dragged him out of the town, up the hill that Nazareth was built on, and would have thrown him over the cliff, but somehow he managed to walk through them and away.

It's an ugly story, one that was to be repeated in Jesus' life when the approval of the Palm Sunday crowd changed to the mood that bayed for his blood only a few days later. And it's an ever-present ugly story, one that would destroy a person or an idea rather than meet its challenge with an open mind. Especially when it comes from a source thought to be known and familiar and reliable. The greatest rage is mostly reserved not for the outsider, but for the one from within who is felt to have sold out, gone over, let the side down, failed to conform.

Where does it come from, this bitter feeling against the one who is known who suddenly acts or speaks in quite a new or different way? We all experience it from time to time, perhaps towards the person who comes along with ideas that upset our preconceived notions about childrearing or working practices or religion. Our hackles rise, and we can hear ourselves mentally saying, 'If it was good enough for his parents, it should be good enough for him', which translates into 'If it was good enough for *my* parents, then it should be good enough for him'. Which in itself translates into 'If it's good enough for me, then it should be good enough for him'. These feelings are not unnatural responses. They come without our bidding when suddenly we are threatened; our carefully carved-out space—*our* way of doing things—is challenged.

And perhaps there's a bit of resentment, of envy, there too. If it's good enough for me, *why* is it not good enough for him? Is he getting something I'm not? Does he know something I don't? Is her life more interesting than mine? And does that therefore make me inferior, stupider, more boring than her? These are not pleasant thoughts, none of us like to have them. And so, in order to cut them off before they really disturb us, it is safer to put up our defences against this new disturbing material. But even if we do that, he's still there with that irritating smile. We have to get rid of him and his pretensions. We have to go on the attack.

We've all been there. We may well have been part of a group that gets infected by this kind of a mood and attacks collectively. Not, of course, that we would ever do anything like trying to throw someone over a cliff. But a little character assassination, a bit of damning with faint praise, a few buckets of cold water thrown on someone's enthusiasms will work wonders. Because most of us do not have the inner confidence that allowed Jesus to stride through the threatening crowd with authority. We are fairly fragile creatures, especially when it comes to risking a new thought or an innovative idea. We can be so easily demoralized, discouraged, undermined.

Yet, in reality, all that we are ever asked to do is to be open, not closed, to the possibility of change and novelty and risk. It is not required of us that we deny our cautious, even fearful, feelings. They are a necessary framework to weigh up the value of the new information. It is more that we need to put them to one side, and not act them out, to reserve judgement until we have given a fair hearing, have really listened to what is new. That also requires of us that we stretch our imaginations somewhat, to visualize not just the worst possible scenario (always easier to do from entrenched territory), but also the best possible one. And it is very rarely anyway that we are challenged to throw away *all* our dearly held beliefs and practices.

Not only does this require an inevitable risk-taking; at least in the imagination, it also requires a decision, a choice. Faced with the overwhelming instinct to close the door, it takes the exercise of some freedom deliberately to hold it open. Threat always evokes a gut reaction, and our gut reactions have their uses, should be taken into account. But we have to be able to discern whether the threat is real or imaginary, whether fear is justified or whether it's actually fear of fear. It's interesting that Jesus, far from being legalistic, never forced people into faith or action. He always left choices and decisions in their hands (sometimes not even waiting around for them to make up their minds), and he resisted all efforts to force him to tell people what to do. But he did unceasingly try to demonstrate, in his words, in his actions, in his person, that the ground of people's being was love, that they were God-encompassed even in strange territory, and therefore they might trust enough to take the odd risk.

But if we attack before we've ever had a really good look at the rider coming over the hill, then we'll never know whether this was a hostile invader, or whether it was actually a messenger coming to invite us to a great feast of tasty dishes in the company of interesting and exotic guests.

One of the problems for all of us is that we know that we don't just step easily from being comfortable and secure at home to being comfortable and secure at the feast. It's not quite that simple. We know that opening ourselves to the new, the unfamiliar, the different, means letting down our defences for a while, means emptying ourselves of the old, the familiar, the known. It means embracing a poverty of knowledge, a recognition of that which we do not know. It means pushing out the limits of what we know to take in, examine, accept for ourselves, and incorporate the new thing. And that's hard work, in which we also recognize a corresponding poverty of spirit that is open to be enlarged. But even if we want to be open, it's hard work, because our limits resist, they push back. There is an innate conservatism in most of us that leads us to defend our territory, even if it's dull and uninteresting, even if it's positively gloomy.

So even if we recognize that in order to grow spiritually we must be constantly stretching our limits, even if we know that if we don't we'll stagnate, it's still hard work, it's still scary to go beyond where we've been and take the first steps towards the great feast.

And yet, we know from the Gospels that there were some folk who had no difficulty at all in moving from where they were, who positively raced towards the feast, who had hardly any inner resistance at all to overcome. Who were these lucky people? Well, they were the lucky tax collectors and prostitutes, the lucky sick and poor, outsiders, children. Of course, 'lucky' is not the appropriate word. Perhaps a better word is 'blessed', in the right place. Not because they were poor or sick or unhappy or alienated. There is no essential value in any of these states, and it's a grave misunderstanding of the gospel to think that any kind of suffering is of itself redemptive. Suffering is mostly damaging and destructive, but its experience often has the effect of making people vulnerable, defenceless, empty.

People who have nothing to lose have nothing to defend. The people who responded to Jesus had no picture of themselves as being good or virtuous or holy. They had no possessions worth hanging on to. They had experienced the vulnerability of illness or of being a stranger in a hostile environment. They had no security of their own—just as children begin with little self-consciousness, no possessions of their own, are vulnerable, and depend on others for their security. These were the people Jesus recognized as being poor in spirit, as knowing their own need. These were the people who raced towards the feast.

No wonder that the Christian gospel has been so attractive to people at the bottom level of many different kinds of society—slaves in America, untouchables in India, peasants in South America. When you have nothing and society tells you that you are nothing, it sounds like good news to hear that the last shall be first, and that you are worth everything.

And children—well, children just take all of life as gift, for with no power, no status, little formal knowledge, all they have they receive. And everything is gift to them—wonderful, curious, delightful—until they grow up and learn other ways, or find that what is given to them is ugly.

Those who are poor and wretched receive the invitation to the feast as gift because they have had everything taken away from them. Children receive it as gift because they have no other way of being. But we—do we experience

life as gift, or are we more inclined to experience it as
lack? We enjoy an affluence and a range of freedoms and
opportunities that would have staggered our grandparents.
Furthermore, the prevailing ideology, whose effects are far
more profound than simply the economic ones, invites us
unceasingly to dwell on what we lack, and to disregard
or find fault with it, and to devalue it. The rhetoric of
capitalism entices us on to a limitless abundance—go for
growth, the world's your oyster, the end of history, no
such thing as society, all you could ever want. Apart
from the lie implicit in this rhetoric (because, in reality,
very few of us are in the position to have everything we
want), and its huge environmental, material, and emotional cost to those whose limits are pushed back ever
more tightly upon them (because, in truth, we share a
small planet whose resources are not infinite), its effect is
so often to thrust us onward to an unsatisfied desire for
permanent fullness, busyness, activity, possession, and
to refuse the experience of emptiness, stillness, lack, as
invalid, unauthentic. And it desensitizes us to the very
real value and worth of what we do in fact have. It is
what Umberto Eco, in *Travels in Hyperreality*, describes
as 'the obsessive determination not to leave a single
space that doesn't suggest something'. And perhaps the
obsession with growth is indeed 'offspring of the unhappy
awareness of a presence without depth'.

This desensitization is often a lack of awareness of the
gifts of the present moment, however small, a blindness
to the blessing of the here and now. I myself find that it
is when I am least sensitive to these small pleasures—sen-
sory, physical, emotional—that I am most likely to grudge
what I don't have, which, paradoxically, makes me more
defensive of my security, less open to new things, and so
less likely to be enriched or surprised. But when I have
a keen sense of the glory of the small things around me,
the chatter of the children, the colour of the sky, the first

21

cup of coffee in the morning, a kind gesture from a friend, and of the fact that all of these are gift, then I am content, then I am not defending, then I am open to receive more of life's mystery with interest and excitement.

꽃ᄋᆞ꽃

OUR REVOLUTION

I like this poem by the American writer Alice Walker:

We alone can devalue gold
by not caring
:ᶜ it falls or rises
..ı the marketplace.
Wherever there is gold
there is a chain, you know,
and if your chain
is gold
so much the worse
for you.

Feathers, shells
and sea-shaped stones
are all as rare.

This could be our revolution:
To love what is plentiful
as much as
what is scarce.

But it's a discipline, a learning (or perhaps an unlearning) that requires hard work, deliberately to set aside our grudges, our hurts, our unsatisfied desires, to lay them down, let them go, and just be empty, full of space, poor in spirit, in order to see what really is in front of our eyes. Some of the hardest work I ever did in my life was spending three months in a place far away from all my friends, my busy working life, and the many attractions of a busy Western city. I had very little money, very little mobility, was in a country where the language and culture were foreign to me, and living in a house that was pleasant, but almost entirely lacking in labour-saving devices. My children and I (for there was no school to fill up their days either) were almost completely dependent on the generosity of others for outings, advice, and information, and much practical support. Some of that was hard for someone used to being in the giving role.

We learned there what was almost a whole new way of being. We learned to cook and enjoy the cheaper local produce, and forgo the expensive, familiar, imported food. We learned to ask for things in another language. Every visitor at the door was eagerly welcomed. Every letter from home was a precious gift. We saw parts of the country and met people we would never otherwise have met, travelling by local buses and walking. A trip to the market or the bakery became a great adventure. An invitation to dinner was indeed an invitation to a great feast. We learned to make works of art with a few strips of plasticine, and rediscovered the joys of imaginative play. I worked hard at finding the positive side of doing all our washing by hand, and in the end I succeeded. When I came home, with red-raw knuckles, I found that my rather temperamental washing-machine—with its tendency to stick and overflow into the bath—was a beautiful sight indeed. We learned to value deeply the generosity of people who never made us feel we were a nuisance in our dependency. But, most of all, we learned a new appreciation of the natural world around us—trees and flowers, birds and sky, sea and insects.

Much of it we learned in the garden of the house we were living in. Each day I spent an hour sitting outside, no book in my hand, no letters to write, no conversations to have. And each day I opened my clenched hand and let go: of thoughts and memories of the past, of hopes and fears for the future, of calculating our expenditure, and anticipating what we would do tomorrow. I let go of hurts and triumphs and theories and solutions, and found some empty space for things to come in. Sights and sounds, smells and sensations.

I felt and smelt (because they all bring smells with them) sun and wind and rain. I saw colour and light and shadow. I heard tiny sounds that I usually miss. But mostly, I encountered insects. Afterwards, I wrote a poem about them:

Now I see skinny lizards, skiting through the grass
and darting geckos,
naked with the vulnerability of rubber bands,
and tiny, twitchy frogs as curious as babies.
I have grown intimate with ants
and carefree with cockroaches.
I hear the whizzing of the dragonfly
above the whirring of the fan.
I have learned to apprehend mosquitoes,
and sat transfixed while butterflies
with wings more beautiful than peacock damask
visited my blue bag time and time again.

A whole and complicated order of creation
imposed itself upon my gaze
while I sat still and drank my coffee
in the garden.
Or rather, I should say,
I opened my eyes and saw it,
opened my ears and heard it,
narrowed my field and selected it.
Together we changed me.

I have an image of a bottle that contains wine to about

halfway up. Some days my bottle is half-empty, and I look at the unfilled bit resentfully, and fiercely guard what I have. Cautious in case I spill even a drop, guarding it so intently that I forget to smell its fruity scent or to appreciate its ruby-red glow, afraid to drink any of it. But some days my bottle is not half-empty, and instead is half-full, and I think that I am blessed—and if I spill a bit, or drink a bit, well, it doesn't matter because I'm enjoying it, and the fullness is a gift, and I can even see the gift in the emptiness. And I think that I am closer to life, and to God, on the days when my bottle is half-full than on the days when it's half-empty. And on these days, I am much more aware of people whose bottle is only a quarter or even a sixteenth full than when I'm caught up with guarding my half-empty bottle.

Maybe the people of Nazareth were having a half-empty day on the day they tried to push Jesus over the cliff rather than really listen to him; the day they were more concerned with seeing themselves reflected in a good light through his eyes than really looking at themselves. But it's a story worth remembering whenever we are tempted to say 'Oh him, I kent his faither.' Perhaps it might help us to reserve judgement—at least until we have made sure that the speaker is not an angel with a message for us!

2

CRYING THE BLUES

Blessed Are the Sorrowful:
They Shall Be Comforted

I never knew Mrs Roberts's first name—or, if I did, I've forgotten it; and at the time when I most needed to remember it, I forgot her surname too. I met her when I was working in the local church in a big housing scheme in Edinburgh, and her name was on a list of people to visit in the parish. Mrs Roberts's husband had been admitted to hospital suffering from brain damage and, though he was unable to speak himself, the church had made contact with his wife through the hospital. Now I had been sent to visit her in her home.

She lived in what must be the biggest stair in Edinburgh. From the one communal entrance, dozens of houses are reached, up to about a seventh floor. The houses do not, as in old-fashioned tenements, share landings. Instead, they open out in rows along draughty, badly lit balconies, opening on one side on to a view across the back of a shopping centre, all overflowing dustbins, running waste pipes, and urinating drunks; over a car park and on towards more square blocks of flats. A gentle flurry of rubbish floats over the scene, and on windy days this becomes a hazard for hurrying people, who are hit by unnameable flying debris, and are tripped up by the newspapers that wrap themselves lovingly around their ankles.

In this depressing landscape, dogs wander, children attempt to play, and women trail bags and toddlers back and forwards to the shops and the social work department. It is a bleak and frightening picture of the conditions of much urban living. On the balconies people do not linger to chat, and neighbours do not pop in to borrow cups of sugar, or have a gossip. Not much of the comforting imagery of slum living remains: not the companionship, the shared hardship, the warmth of human relationships, nor the sense of belonging that persists against all the odds in the old inner-city areas. There is no pride of place. Only thousands of people living as closely as ever, but cautious, fearful, contained behind heavily bolted doors. When I knocked on Mrs Roberts's door, a small, thin, tentative woman with a tired face answered. She seemed pleased to see me, if a bit taken aback, and invited me in.

She made me a cup of tea and told me her story—diffidently at first, because it was a story of shame and violence. She had lived there for sixteen years, after moving from the old part of the city where she grew up. She had two children, a boy of fifteen and a girl of thirteen, who both went to the local school. She worked as a packer in a factory that employed many of the women in the area. Her husband had quite a good job in a nearby electronics firm—again, a large employer for the neighbourhood.

She talked about her husband, and gradually I gained a picture of a withdrawn and gloomy man who suffered from long spells of depression. He spent a lot of time in the local pub, a place that at times resembled a Wild West saloon, both in the utter dismalness of its appearance and in its air of lawlessness; it was a place where fights regularly took place, drugs changed hands, and any woman who went there was assumed to be no better than she should be. (My husband once went in there soon after we moved

27

to the area. He was alone, wearing a sweatshirt, jeans, and a pair of clogs. He entered the public bar, and a silence fell upon the place as all eyes turned on him. Then out of the silence came a slow hissing, and the whispered word 'poof'. My husband did not stop to chat!)

Though Mrs Roberts's husband was not a gregarious man, he was inclined to become aggressive and loud after he had had a lot to drink. One night, he had gone there as usual, and Mrs Roberts was at home, as usual, doing the housework, watching television. Much later, the police came to the door to tell her that her husband had been involved in a fight with the manager of the pub, and had been taken to hospital. When she got to the hospital she discovered that he had been hit so hard with a brick or stone that it had taken a huge lump out of his head. He was now in a coma, unable to speak or move, with only his eyes still showing signs of life. And so he remained until he died, two years later.

There was much confusion about what had happened. The bar manager was a tough and violent man, much given to threat and suspected of many kinds of illegal activity, so the police seized on this opportunity to press charges against him. But it seemed that Mr Roberts had acted belligerently, had threatened him, had possibly initiated the fight. In any case, he was not a popular man, and there were few who would speak up in his defence. The case came to trial and the manager was found not guilty.

It dragged through the papers for days, and each day Mrs Roberts suffered as her husband, now a comatose shell, was described in every fault and deficiency of character. It must have been—was, I could see (for at this time I saw her almost every day)—agony for her, alone but for her children and with little support from relatives or friends, to witness her husband's humiliation, and hers too, for it was not a story that originated in happy married life. And each day she had to go to her shift in the factory, and face the curiosity, gossip, and casual sympathy of the women she worked with.

For a year her husband remained in a ward for severely brain-damaged patients, and she visited him two or three times a week, sitting by his bed, talking to him only when his eyes flickered. Then he was moved, this time to a hospital outside of the city for people who were not expected to respond to treatment, and so her visits were accompanied by a tedious two-hour bus journey. But she continued to visit him faithfully. Eventually, having never regained consciousness, he died.

All this time, I visited her regularly, and we built up an unusual relationship. It was in no sense equal. I only ever saw her in her house, and we talked mainly of her concerns, though she knew something of my life and would ask for my husband every time we met. It could hardly be termed a friendship, but it lacked both the direction and the clarity to qualify as a professional/client relationship. She was not a member of the church, and never attended; she never asked for advice or help or prayer. I was just someone who came to call, a weekly version of the stranger on the train. I cannot imagine that an inexperienced twenty-five-year-old, groping for ways in which to express solidarity, can have been of much use to her. And yet each week, sometimes for two or three hours at a stretch, we talked with a depth and honesty that I have rarely encountered since. If I say that this woman and I talked about philosophy, theology, politics, and spirituality, it may sound pretentious and silly. But it is true.

She never complained or bemoaned her lot. What had her life been—a childhood lived in grey poverty; a home in a place where to live marks you out in the eyes of many as a failure; work that was insecure (the women were always speculating about short-time working, redundancy, closure), monotonous, and futile. Children who, a source of pleasure when small, were now also a source of anxiety—the girl because she was lazy, feckless, and loud, always in trouble at school, and only interested in boys; the boy, who was sensitive, intelligent, and yet withdrawn like his father, a fish out of water in school and with other boys. And a marriage that had started with all the hopes and dreams and enthusiasms of most marriages, but had gone sour and stale, two people living side by side in isolation and frustration, ending in humiliation and death.

Her greatest pleasure now was the Saturday shopping expedition to the old part of town where she had been brought up. She still did all her shopping in this area, three miles and a bus journey away, had done so for sixteen years. She was, I suppose, in her early forties, and her life, to me observing it, seemed to represent all the waste, dreariness, and hopelessness that I most feared for my own life. It was a life that looked like hell to me, bereft of beauty, meaning, and purpose. It would always be possible to point to other, more extreme, more dramatic, instances of human suffering, but it was my deepest and most profound experience of the graveyard of human hopes.

And yet she did not act as a victim. She did not speak unkindly of her neighbours, her husband, her family, nor even of the man who had killed her husband. She did not rage against fate or God or herself. Instead, she tried to understand. She struggled, tentatively and painfully, to understand why people behaved in the way they did, what drove them, what brought them to the point of cruelty or indifference. She tried to understand her relationship with her husband, where it had gone wrong, at what point they had stopped communicating, the frustration that pushed him into depression, alcohol, and despair. Though they had ceased to know each other long before, her spirit still cared about him, lying motionless in his bed, and she entered in her imagination into his suffering. She did not judge, either herself or others, but accepted her life in its entirety, not thinking it to have been good, not thinking it to have been just, not fatalistically as if she had no right to expect anything better, but as something given—simply as life.

From time to time she would remember moments, occasions, that had been precious. Very simple, they were: walks with her husband and children; a holiday outing; the early days of her marriage. And from time to time, she would look forward, make little plans for a trip with a friend, something new for the house. Often she talked about the world: about its suffering; the senselessness of war; the need for people to share things more. And sometimes she talked about her regrets, her fears, her dreams, and she too wanted her life to mean something, to be of value.

I tried to say that I thought her life *was* valuable, not particularly for anything she said or did, but just because of the person she was. I think she had too much humility to take me seriously, and anyway I don't suppose I put it very well. But this wee thin woman, who had all the reason in the world to be bitter, was kind and good and strong, and full of sorrow for others in their pain. At cost, she kept her spirit alive, looking into the future with anxiety and into the past with regret, and always trying to understand, to know her sorrow. And yet, with great endurance, entering into the life of the present, keeping it going, keeping her hope alive.

A few months after her husband died, I saw her again unexpectedly—at the Christmas service in the church. Not the midnight service, when all those who didn't usually come to church attended, but the 10 a.m. service, only attended by a few. She had never been in the

31

church before, though we had talked a lot about God and Christianity. I felt that in some way she was giving something to me, doing something that meant a great deal to me. At the door on the way out, she came up with the others to greet me. I knew so well who she was, and yet for one awful moment my mind went completely blank and I could not think of her name to call her by it. 'Mrs Roberts,' she said shyly, and I nodded and shook her hand and smiled at her, and then she passed on in the crowd. Shortly afterwards, we moved away. I have not seen her since that time.

I hope that she has found peace in her refusal to give way to bitterness, and in the daily life that she has lived with such endurance. I hope that she has found consolation in her children. I hope that her spirit, which she had the courage to explore, has been comforted.

WILL THE CIRCLE BE UNBROKEN?

I've only ever been to one proper wake, and it was for Brian. Brian was a member of the resident staff living in Iona Abbey, where I was the warden with my husband. He worked as the secretary of the Iona Prayer Circle (an intercessory network of prayer for healing), although he was a teacher of handicapped children by profession. He died in his room in the Abbey, after a three-year struggle with cancer. He was thirty-five years old, with a wife and three children.

At the wake, which was held in a room decorated for a party with candles and flowers, there was food: lentil soup, ham and salad, and bread and cakes—good, homely Scots fare of the kind that will absorb alcohol and grief. There was wine and whisky. The children were all there, as they had been throughout his illness, both his own and the other Abbey children. Lots of people sang songs, and one person performed a virtuoso turn on the bagpipes—musical and funny and irreverent. Anna, Brian's widow, and her sisters wore red carnations, and they sang too. I still have a tape of that singing, and it was beautiful because they were all good singers, and because they were singing their sorrow and their relief and their pity.

After a while, someone put the lights out and lit a candle for Brian. We all stood in a circle and passed the light from hand to hand. When you got the candle, you held it for a minute, and if you wanted to say something about him, share a memory, paint a picture of him at a time you remembered, then you could. If you didn't want to do that, then you could just pass it on to the next person. As the candle went round, and lit each face in turn, it was like a montage of relationships. It was as if Brian's spirit and the spirit of each person merged in a story. Brian and Anna, Brian and the children, Brian and his mother, his colleagues, his friends, Brian and the people who had heard him sing. The Holy Spirit, the go-between God, moved among us, drawing us into communion, the communion of the saints.

The moments were precious to the people who had experienced them. But behind many of them there was pain—the pain of a singing voice that had grown weak with illness, the pain of a nightmare journey in an ambulance, the pain of hospital bureaucracy and professional ineptitude and indifference, the pain of a friend with flesh falling away and the indignity of weakness, the pain of the morphine struggle, the pain of a life not perfect, and not loved perfectly, but loved greatly, the pain of a life cut short of so many good things. And then it seemed as if all our pain came marching up to stand behind his pain—broken marriages, dead babies, betrayed friendships, fear of dying, doubt, failure, guilt, torment, all standing there in solidarity with Brian's pain beyond the gilded memories. And beyond even the pain, in that moment of absolute silence when the circle was complete, and only for that moment, the peace that passes understanding.

Later on, Laurie sang 'Victor Jara', the song that more than any other I associated with Brian, and for a moment I felt pure shock and protest. Then I thought that it was right that the song should be carried on, even though the singer was dead, and that Laurie should sing it. Apart from anything else, that was the spirit in which Victor Jara lived. It was 'life flowing on in endless song amid earth's lamentations', and it was not crude or cynical. One of Anna's sisters told me that long ago in the West of Ireland each singer or fiddler had an air, a carolan, that belonged to him alone, and that when he died no one ever played it again and it was forgotten. But not the songs that Brian sang. They were about a continuing struggle.

Brian's funeral service was one of words and music and drama and procession, and he had been welcomed back to the earth with a crack of thunder and then a drenching rain to mingle his ashes with the earth. At that service, the mourners had given Brian back to the mystery from which he had come. We had celebrated his life and death, and acknowledged that beyond here, his spirit went where human beings do not go. In our prayers, we had passed his spirit from its place among the spirits that are ours to its place in the spirit that is distinct. We commended his spirit to God, and committed his mortal remains to the earth.

At the wake, we gave expression to our sorrowing spirits. We opened them to the experience of sorrow and loss. We made a space for them to be touched by our knowledge of Brian. And they were touched, not just in their knowledge of him, but in all the pain and joy of our own self-knowledge.

'WHY HAVE YOU ABANDONED ME?'

As I said, I have only ever been to one wake. But many times I have taken tea after a funeral—in discreet hotels where funeral suppers are 'respectfully catered for'; in public houses where the fare is more solid and you can drown your sorrows; in front rooms in council houses and bungalows, where neighbours bring cakes and relatives meet, perhaps for the first time in years. At a few, but only a few, of these occasions, have people been able to give expression to their sorrowing spirits. More often, they have felt it necessary to suppress them instead. In order not to upset the widow or make unseemly displays of emotion, they mutter conventional words of sympathy, sit dumb for a few minutes, then turn with relief to intense conversations about house prices or football, or to catching up with the cousin from London. Sometimes it turns into a maudlin, sentimental occasion with all the attention turned on Uncle Willie, who is disgracing himself with drink, or into an unpleasant scene where the claws come out, and stick into all those who didn't do their duty by the dead when they were living, but have the gall to turn up to the funeral. We greet death in these ways, not through badness, but mostly just because these are the options that are open to us. But sometimes, warm after the chill of cemetery or crematorium, comfortable among friends, disarmed by emotion, I have seen it happen in the most conventional of settings, that meeting of sorrowing spirits.

When the wake was more commonplace, when the knowledge of death itself was more commonplace, it must have been easier for it to happen. But it is harder now, because all our conditioning, all our conventions, teach us that it is wrong, even shameful, to be sorrow-full. Laugh and the world laughs with you, weep and you weep alone; not necessarily because people don't care, but because we don't know how to deal with sorrow. It's common for people who have been bereaved to find that friends avoid them, are uncomfortable in their company, begin to treat them a little differently. Our culture has a tendency to sweep anything painful under the carpet—illness, death, endings, partings, tensions. There is no adequate way to deal with human sorrow, of course. But we are discouraged from even accepting it as an inescapable fact of life. Covering it up, glossing it over, escaping from it in work, these are acceptable. But confronting sorrow is often deeply embarrassing for us, for those around us. So we have been anaesthetized in our society; our senses are numbed. And when the cry of anguish wells up from within us—'My God, my God, why have you abandoned me?'—we push it down again. And sometimes, the last place the cry will be heard is in the church, with its relentless drive to obliterate sorrow, anger, and raw hurt in the platitudes of doctrine.

Pushing the cry down, we deny the way life is, the way we are—lost, grieving, mortal. It's hard to confront our limits. We are not in control, we are always facing our own death and all the little deaths: of dreams, of relationships, of our own self-image.

But pushing the cry down may push us into great depression and despair. Deprived of our cry, we have to deprive ourselves also of its causes. If it is wrong to feel abandoned, then we must be at fault, there must be something wrong with us, we must be being punished. The prison of no release from our sorrow, no escape from our pain, closes around us.

To deny sorrow is not necessarily the brave act of will we sometimes admire. The turning away is also a turning away from the ability to discern threat, so that it becomes

36

possible to contemplate with resignation huge human suffering and, with fatalistic acceptance, the dismantling of the life-support systems our planet depends on for its existence. Resignation and denial are passive—but sorrow is active, dynamic. It moves us on.

If we turn away from the expression of our sorrowing spirits, we also turn away from the possibility of the deepest joy. If we do not live with the reality of death, then we are denied the true experience of life. It is a cliché to say that those people who have had a narrow escape from death experience life as very sweet. But we all escape death narrowly every day. Our lives are slender threads in the hand of mystery, and the beginning and end of the threads are part of the whole.

I am not talking about the perverse seeking out of pain that has sometimes passed for sorrow in religion—the extreme asceticism, the mortification of the flesh, the glorification of abasement. Nor am I talking of making a virtue out of necessity. We cannot say to anyone who has lost child or lover, been starved or degraded, anything but that you would it had been otherwise. But we cannot live lives that are sufficient unto themselves, however much we want to. We are, by virtue of our common humanity, our mortal condition, bound together. Both personally, in the common human experiences of everyday living, and corporately, when we enter into the tragedy of the human condition, the cup of sorrow awaits us.

Spirituality is not tended or healed through the denial of a profound facet of human existence. The cry 'Why have you abandoned me?'—whether addressed to God or to fate, to the mother who did not love us enough or the father who deserted us, to the lover who did not want us or to the child who grew up and went away, or even to the child in us who once saw the magic in the world—that cry must be expressed, for only then can it be answered.

It is a cry that comes when we are feeling weak, unable to cope, confused, scared, alone. It will come when we have least resource, least power. It may come when we have to cope with family dependency, uncaring agencies, cynical publicity. As we struggle with what it means to live and die, which the death of others or our own illness has forced us to do, we will go searching for immortality, choose to refuse the fact of our death. We may be experiencing thoughts and feelings that we have no way of interpreting or understanding. We may be 'tired of living and scared of dying'. But we cannot afford to stifle the cry. Only when we make space for our sorrowing spirits will we be comforted.

'TO BE MADE STRONG'

Comfort is another word which has had a bad press. It so often seems like an escape word, a selfish word, perhaps because we associate it with armchairs and affluence. But it actually means 'to be made strong', to be strengthened. Strengthened to endure, to respond, to change?

A few years ago I went to Okinawa, the island that is now part of Japan, where the final battles in the Pacific were fought during the Second World War. While I was there I visited the vast catacomb of caves where the Japanese army made its last stand. An Okinawan woman, who as a young girl had been pressed into service as a nurse to the Japanese casualties, told me how, when it became obvious that defeat was inevitable, the Japanese soldiers were ordered to commit hara-kiri, ritual suicide, in their thousands. As Japanese, as soldiers, their traditional loyalty was to the Emperor, and they were honour-bound to die gloriously with his name on their lips. But, she said, most of them did not die like that. They were scared, suffering, trapped (if they did not commit suicide, they were put to death). And they were sorrowful. At that moment, all nationalism, all thoughts of defeat and glory faded away, and they died with a cry on their lips. They cried for their mothers, their wives, their children. I hope that in their inevitable deaths they were strengthened in their sorrow by their cries. The woman who had watched them believed it.

At Brian's wake, we had the rare and precious opportunity to make our cry of sorrow together. And in so doing, we were profoundly strengthened and comforted, and even knew peace. It was not a permanent comfort or peace, for nothing is permanent, but it was a promise, an intimation, a sign that these things were possible and would come again. For two years, Mrs Roberts made her cry to me, for it began while her husband lay in hospital, dead to her in any life they had had. Together, we held a wake that lasted for two years.

I remember a man coming to stay in the Abbey of Iona shortly after the death of his wife who was in her forties. Near the end of his stay, he came to me and asked if we had ever considered having in the Abbey what he termed a 'book of life'. For, he said, famous people are remembered, and their deaths are marked. But there should be somewhere to write down the lives of ordinary people and mark their deaths. He had loved his wife greatly, she had been a lovely and good woman, though she was an ordinary person.

There should be wakes, there should be books, there should be ways in which sorrow may be allowed to possess our spirits, and our spirits may stand in communion with those whose spirits have gone where ours cannot follow, and with the spirits of others who share our sorrow. Then the communion of saints will not just be a pious phrase, but an experienced reality, and the sorrowful shall be comforted.

3

COMING DOWN TO EARTH

Blessed Are the Humble:
They Shall Inherit the Earth

❧❦·❧❦

May was born in 1888, the same year as Adolf Hitler. She was the youngest of eight children, born when her father, an Ayrshire farmer, was in late middle age. She grew up on the shores of beautiful Loch Long (now a huge nuclear naval base) in a house called Albert Park to which her parents had retired. Long before she reached adolescence, her brothers had grown up and gone, scattered to the corners of the globe in the way of so many young Scotsmen, lured by the prospects that British imperialism opened up to them—one to Australia, another to Canada, another to die young in South Africa. Her closest relationships were with her sisters, close to her in age and in the experience of late Victorian girlhood. When her father died, she and her mother and sisters moved to a flat in a sandstone tenement in the West End of Glasgow. There they took into their home as lodgers students from the nearby University of Glasgow.

Beautiful middle-class Edwardian Glasgow, living side by side with grimy, overcrowded, insanitary industrial Glasgow. City of glorious pink buildings, spacious flats overlooking trees and gardens (like the bourgeois life of Paris and Vienna and Berlin), walks in the Botanic Gardens and through the Kibble Palace (a grandly named hothouse), or along quiet streets that suddenly disappeared up steep hills where houses of extraordinarily Bohemian character materialized unexpectedly as if they would disappear once passed; of shopping in Byers Road and churchgoing in one of the great plush-seated churches that abounded in the area; of tearooms and bridge parties. And the quietest of lives: school till only fourteen (for she was a girl, and not academic), then at home helping Mother.

In 1911 she married Bertie, a young minister of the Church of Scotland, son of a Glasgow grocer. Bertie and May. They seem like names from an era long past, bearing no relation to the world we now inhabit. And yet she lived to see the atomic bomb dropped on Hiroshima, to fly the Atlantic in six hours, and to see men land on the moon. The newlyweds honeymooned on Loch Lomond, setting out from the reception in a pony and trap, driving round the lochside with ribbons streaming from the driver's whip. From there, they went to their first home in Dumbarton, an industrial Clydeside town made great from shipbuilding, and they did not leave it again for thirty-seven years, when Bertie died after a lifetime's work in one parish.

In Dumbarton they lived through the Great War and the rise of Red Clydeside, through the General Strike and the Depression years that followed, through the Second World War and the birth of the Welfare State. They had four sons born between 1914 and 1922, and by 1942 they were all in uniform—one as a chaplain in a Scottish army regiment in Europe, one in the Fleet Air Arm in the Far East, one in an RAF aircrew, and one a lieutenant in the Argyll and Sutherland Highlanders in Malaya. This last, named after his father, was reported missing, presumed dead in the forests of Malaya at the age of twenty-three. There is a photograph of him in his uniform, kilt and glengarry, smiling and moustached and charming. His body was never recovered.

To live in Dumbarton from 1911 to 1948 was to live in a place that experienced the turbulence of these years in its heart. A town of young men who went to the trenches of Flanders, a shipbuilding town that took the very worst of the Depression, a labour town that was a seedbed for unrest and idealism, a tough town that downed tools during the General Strike, a naval town that was a target for some of the worst bombing of Britain during the Second World War, a poor town that needed the Welfare State. As a pastor in an industrial parish, Bertie must have visited homes of great poverty, comforted many families that, like his own, had lost loved ones during the war, sat with men and women grey with the fatigue and worry of strikes, unemployment, divided loyalties. As a citizen, he would be aware of great and serious issues—patriotism, nationalism, war, and the struggle between capital and labour. And through all these years, May (who never had a paid job and would have been horrified at the thought) looked after the manse, raised the children, baked, opened fund-raising events, welcomed her sons' friends, visited parishioners, and opened her home to innumerable visitors of every description—from the professional people who lived around the manse to the gaunt families of unemployed shipbuilders.

After the war, with her remaining sons either at university, or married and following their profession (they all became ministers like their father), May devoted more of her energies to caring for her husband, who had become badly crippled and now conducted services from his wheelchair. In anticipation of his retirement they bought a small terraced house in Helensburgh, a pleasant dormitory town on the Clyde coast. But Bertie died before he had ever lived in it, so she moved there by herself. Here she lived for the next eighteen years, rarely alone, for she was always having folk to stay, her family, her friends, friends of her family, and family of her friends. She welcomed them all to her little house, often giving up her bed to sleep on a sofa bed in the sitting room, perhaps with a grandchild tucked in beside her. For many, many people, her home became a kind of sanctuary, a base for bracing walks along the Esplanade and freezing dips in the open-air swimming pool, for visits to the tearoom and picnics in Glen Fruin, where ammunition dumps have now closed it off to the public. To a whole generation of children, many quite unrelated to her, and to their parents as well, she was Granny Orr.

I remember her house vividly: the brass knocker and the brass plate for letters in the hall; the Indian carpet and the old sofa with its pink silk cushions in the sitting room; the dark dining room with the old-fashioned cruet and fragile china alongside the plastic plates and beakers; the tiny scullery/kitchen with no refrigerator, only a small gauze-covered icebox; the back porch with the battered wicker chairs and buckets and spades and umbrellas; the nasturtiums in the minute square back garden. I remember lounging around with lots of cousins on the beds under the sloping roofs in one of the two low bedrooms upstairs. I remember lying at night in the sofa bed in the sitting room, always with someone lying beside me, listening to footsteps clacking past in the street, and wondering about the world, and trying (and failing) to imagine the stars going on for ever. I remember being taken by her to the public library, which was situated in an old house, and, with the sunlight streaming on to the wood panelling and an endless supply of books, experiencing a moment of the utmost happiness, a feeling of such profound sanctuary that it seemed as if the world itself loved me, and cared for me, and wanted me to be happy.

By the time she reached her mid-seventies, she had decided that it was right to move once again (and she obviously knew it would be for the last time). May moved back into Glasgow, to just a few streets away from her girlhood home. This last move took her to sheltered housing run by the church, which combined care and companionship with a measure of independence. Next door to the building was a hostel for girls, and May always enjoyed inviting a few of them, often far from their homes in the highlands or islands, to come and have tea with her. I remember her making meringues for two of these girls, to whom she had also become Granny Orr.

She continued to lead a busy and sociable life. As well as the regular round of outings, church events, and visitors, she often travelled to stay with family and friends; she set off on a bus with her small weekend bag, her handbag, and a net bag full of a treasury of sweets, letters, papers, and indigestion tablets. She was an intrepid traveller, this old lady now well into her late seventies, setting off dauntlessly to traverse the country from Border to Highland, quite alone, always on public transport, self-sufficient, creating her own environment of welcome and comfort round about her.

At the age of seventy-seven, she left her native country for the first time, and flew, also for the first time, to Canada to visit one of her sons who had settled there with his family. She made many friends. When she left, I suppose she imagined it unlikely that she would make the trip again, and it must have been hard for her to say goodbye to this son, and the three beloved granddaughters. Shortly afterwards, she received news that her son had been killed in a car crash. He had been alone. Thus she outlived a second son.

Perhaps this was a blow that took too much out of her. Perhaps her wonderfully healthy body, which had never been in a hospital, and whose greatest irritation seemed to be varicose veins and corns on the toes, was just wearing out. She had a mild heart attack and, though she recovered, her level of activity had of necessity to ease to a gentler pace. But people continued to visit, and she still took her regular trips to drink coffee and meet friends.

She died on the last day of April on a clear sunny morning. She had gone to stay with two elderly distant cousins in Ayrshire. They brought her breakfast in bed and the morning paper. She died very peacefully reading the *Glasgow Herald*. I expect she was reading the Births, Marriages, and Deaths at the time. It would have been characteristic. She was buried in the company of friends beside her husband under long grasses and overgrown shrubs in a Dumbarton cemetery.

It is the story of a very ordinary life, a life like that of millions of others who were born in an age of empire, lived through two world wars, and died in the nuclear age—all without ever being remarked upon. It is the story of a woman who was horrified by notions of women's liberation, yet was happy to support the professional aspirations of her granddaughters. A woman who lived all her life close to great political and social issues, in a town that made socialists of at least two of her sons, and yet resolutely voted Conservative because 'that's what Grandpa voted'. A woman whose reading matter was confined to the *Sunday Post*, the *People's Friend* and the novels of D. E. Stevenson, but whose advice was sought by many more scholarly. A woman of the middle class, who yet experienced real financial hardship (at one stage, she sold off the fragile china) and the kind of insecurity known to all clergy without a private income—at least until very recently. A woman whose life was in some respects sheltered, yet who suffered the bombing of her home, the death of a son in war, the devastation of a whole way of life, and who mixed with people from every sector and condition of society. All contradictions, paradoxes—just like everyone's life contains, of course. But these are not the things I, or other people, remember about her.

I remember that she was the most classless person I ever met. She treated everyone exactly the same, either as friends or as potential friends. She approached them with the same warmth and in the same manner and with the same expectation that they had only been waiting for this opportunity to tell her the story of their lives. Which, to their surprise, most of them had. She cared not at all for her surroundings, but accepted each as yet another chance to talk to all the interesting people around her. Bus station, surgery, hospital, church, shop, street—she would talk to anyone anywhere! Not because she had made some sort of decision, but because she could not do otherwise. She fed them pandrops and cups of coffee out of her little flask and wrapped them around in the warmth of her complete attention to them. The most unexpected people poured out their troubles to her, and she listened and gave sensible, motherly advice. Her family used to joke about the people she would pick up, some of whom would write letters or turn up at the door. She never forgot a name, even of people she had met decades before, and the small details of family connections were the stuff of life for her, because they were just that, connections, the links that held people together, the threads that wove them into belonging in the web of life.

She wasn't perfect, of course. She could be irritating, slow, set in her ways. But I suppose that what all the men and women and children she drew to her experienced was that sense of shelter, of sanctuary, of being utterly at home with her immediately. Her interest in them did not spring from any sense of benevolence or duty or of being a good Christian. She had no great idea of her own importance. She just found people of the utmost interest and delight, and showed it. She didn't judge them or try to impose her own agenda on them. She just took them as she found them. She was a humble and gentle woman with an enormous talent for friendship, which she nurtured to the full. I imagine there are many people who have, or had, a grandmother like that.

❦ · ❦

THE POLITICS OF DIRT

In the place where I lived when my children were babies, men didn't hang out washing. It was considered an unmanly thing to do, even if you were unemployed and at home all day, even if your wife went out to work. It was a constant source of entertainment to our neighbour to look over the fence and see my children's father and the man next door (who also did it) hanging out long lines of wet clean nappies. You may never have thought of it in this way, but dirt is a subject that is high on the agenda of gender politics.

Domestic dirt is still, for the most part, a woman's affair. Even though we are supposed to live in an era of greater equality between the sexes, this is one area where the myth outstrips the reality, as studies consistently show. Women still carry the primary responsibility for cleaning the house, the clothes, and, where they are unable to do it for themselves, the people. Many women's whole lives are given over to this task. Women are also responsible, by and large, for dirt management in public places. Hospitals, schools, and offices are cleaned by women. In eating and drinking places, lines become more blurred though, for men wash dishes in restaurants and mop floors in bars.

Demarcation returns, however, when you go outside. Men clean cars. Men sweep the streets and collect the rubbish, and it's obviously considered as unwomanly for women to sweep streets as it is unmanly for men to hang out the washing, because in this country, you don't see many women doing it (this may be partly explained by the fact that domestic dirt is often dealt with in tandem with looking after children, sick people, and the very old). And men dispose of the bodily dirt we all create: they run the sewage plants and unblock the drains, and they bury our remains when we die. There's such a lot of dirt everywhere that it keeps a large part of the population fully occupied in dealing with it. Of course, stereotypes are breaking down, and many men hang out washing, and women wash cars and unblock drains. Still, though, dirt remains a very big part of life, perhaps the biggest for a lot of people.

Humble people know that life is dirty. Humble people don't despise other people for the dirt they produce. Humble people just get on and deal with it. Even the name suggests an affinity with dirt. The word 'humus', from which 'humble' is derived, simply means 'of the earth, earthy'. Many, though not all, humble people are poor. One of the attractions of being rich is that it helps you to get away from dirt. If you are rich, you can put your left-over food down a waste disposal unit, and have superelectronic washing-machines to get rid of the dirt in your clothes (or send them to the cleaners). You can use lots of gadgets to keep your house clean (of course, these things have other attractions also). Or you can pay someone else to come and do the whole thing for you. You can live in a big house with a big garden instead of in a crowded street. You can travel by car instead of bus. It's easier to keep dirt at bay if you are rich: in your hospitals, your streets, your home. There are less people to make a mess.

Of course, there are many advantages of technology to offset the high energy costs with their concomitant environmental costs, and also the fact that they do tend to work to the advantage of the already better-off. There are decided gains in terms of time saved, drudgery spared, and the opportunities they offer to people to do more creative things, earn more money, and so on. And clean places and people are more attractive than dirty ones. Nevertheless, there are some interesting value judgements about dirt that underlie much of its management. The most obvious one is that almost invariably it is accorded an incredibly low status.

Even for rich people, it's easier for men to escape dirt than women. One of the big differences between men and women in this division of dirt is that only some men are allocated the task of dealing with a bit of it, while most women have to deal with it every day. Even dealing with their own dirt is more value-free for men than for women. Historically, women have been considered and taught to think of themselves as 'unclean' druing menstruation, have been more closely identified with 'matter', while men have been identified more with the spiritual, the intellectual, the rational.

And away from gender politics, there are societies where whole groups of people have been set aside by birth to be the ones who deal with dirt. And these are the groups at the very bottom of the social strata. Even in the West, cleaning jobs are either extremely badly paid and unprotected (in the public sphere), or invisible (in the domestic sphere) and, again, low in status.

Perhaps because it has been more in the daily lot of women to deal with dirt, being humble has been seen more as a female characteristic or quality. It would certainly make it much more difficult and offensive to sluice excrement off a baby's nappy or the bedsheet of an incontinent old person with an inflated sense of one's own importance, a feeling that somehow such a task was beneath one's dignity. Feeling like that might either be a feeling that dirt is somehow unnatural, alien, or it might be a feeling that there is something wrong, bad, about nature because it includes dirt.

To feel that dirt is unnatural is to deny the reality of the way life is. It is to deny the reality of the body, which must sweat, urinate, and defecate (as well as breathe, drink, and eat) in order to stay alive. It is to deny the reality of one's procreation (inter urinas et faeces) and one's birth, when blood and semen play a vital part, and of one's existence, which may well include eating dead flesh and drinking the mother's milk of other animals; our sustenance and the very air we breathe come from a ceaseless round of growth and decay.

Not, of course, that there's anything new about these feelings. In the second century AD, the Gnostics asserted that Jesus 'ate and drank but did not defecate', because it so offended them to imagine that someone so good should have to empty his bowels. For the same reason, men have despised their own bodies, and even more the bodies of women, for being dirty; have flagellated and starved themselves; have raped, mutilated, and burned to punish themselves for being bodily.

And women have all too often taken into themselves this negative picture of their bodies, and of the processes of the body, and have either felt utterly guilty about carnality and fleshliness, or have adopted the prevailing cultural image of the acceptable female body and have manipulated and sometimes mutilated their own bodies in an effort to make them conform to this, the only female image that they can feel good about. From the footbinding of China to the cosmetic self-sculpting of California to the various eating disorders that affect thousands of particularly young women, females have been denied the power and beauty of their naturally diverse bodies in ways that are often painful and sometimes dangerous.

From there, it is often only a small step to using 'dirty' as an indicator of inferiority, unnaturalness, on a large scale; to attacking 'dirty niggers' or the 'dirty' Indians or gypsies or Jews or the 'dirty queers'—anyone who by virtue of their physical attributes or cultural differences or their art reminds us of that which we would rather forget or deny or attribute to others: that we too have bodies, are carnal, are dirty.

On the other hand, the feeling that dirt is indeed natural, but that that then makes nature bad (because dirt is bad), is equally damaging. We would have little respect for nature. We might hold creation in contempt, and we would then feel free to treat it with carelessness, to tear up its soil and decimate its forests, poison its air and waters, and threaten it in a thousand different ways. We would make war on it, and treat it like an enemy to be plundered. We might even do the same thing to the nature we demonstrate in our own being and our own experience: declare war on it. We might decide that the good part of us is the part that is above bodily concerns and instincts, and so repress them, attempting to defeat these feelings with strict discipline and self-denial. We might be very harsh with ourselves, with our feelings and desires, because they would always represent something that was intrinsically bad. We might attempt only to think about and do what we believed are the good and beautiful things, and they would therefore be things that are separate from ordinary dirty life. We might separate love from its very fleshly expressions, and search always for romance, beauty, perfection in relationships. We might venerate the 'intellectual', the 'spiritual', uncontaminated by the emotional, the irrational, the intuitive, and look down on people who allow their judgement to be 'clouded' by feeling. We would be people of principles, of absolutes, of extremes.

Or we might (believing dirt to be both natural and bad) fear nature for its power, its ability to make people do things against their expressed beliefs or better judgement, for its 'dark forces'. We might even make an idol out of nature, a vengeful god needing to be placated, requiring

51

tribute at regular intervals in order to buy time to pursue higher things in safety. There are many, particularly perhaps women, who make sacrifices on that altar, who give their labour to hold back the power of dirt for another few hours, hours in which they can hold on to the picture of themselves as the perfect housewife. But it is a fearful god that can never be entirely appeased and always lurks, ready to strike with ferocity when the window-cleaner discovers an unmade bed, or a neighbour surprises a sinkful of dirty dishes.

Of course, these are extremes, caricatures even, and nowadays we think that rational people have moved away from these somewhat primitive extremes. And even where we see such attitudes still displayed, we know that their holding is not usually a matter of choice, but of a whole complex mixture of childhood experiences, cultural conditioning, and unexamined prejudices. But they are, I think, attitudes worth considering and questioning. After all, we still live in a society where advertising for sanitary towels (used regularly for many years by half the population) provokes an outraged storm, where a breastfeeding woman can be told, in a not very public place, 'How can you do that where people might see you, it's disgusting', and where one of the worst forms of insult is still 'You're a dirty . . .'.

The fear or denial of the physical, whether bodies with their functions and instincts, or that projected on to the earth itself, is destructive, ugly, and deeply unnatural. Small children do not have it unless and until they are taught it. In Christian terms, it is a denial of incarnation, embodiment. In the Christian Church, the theology that split the material and the physical from the spiritual has caused untold harm, and has been used to justify and sanctify poverty, cruelty, and misery. Our spirituality, our profoundest motivations, are *always* expressed and made manifest in and through the physical.

We have a tendency in our society to use the term 'materialist' as a derogatory one, a put-down of someone we think is lacking in 'spiritual values', who grasps and clutches at things for status, security, meaning. But perhaps the problem is not that we are too materialist—perhaps we are not materialist enough. Grasping and clutching, after all, show little respect or reverence for the intrinsic nature of the thing desired. Alan Watts has written: 'A materialist is a person who loves material—wood and leather, flax and silk, eggs and fruit, stone and glass, fish and bread, olives and wine . . .' A materialism that can love the stoneness of stone and the wateriness of water, the fleshiness of flesh and the bloodiness of blood *for its own sake* is perhaps happier to appreciate and let be than a possessiveness that exploits these for so-called 'spiritual purposes'.

But earthy people, carnal people, humble people, do not feel that dirt is unnatural. They do not feel that dirt is bad. Humble people feel that dirt is dirt. Inescapably there, part of us, and we of it, inextricably tied up with the splendour as well as the squalor of life. Humble people are on good terms with dirt. They have demythologized it, whether consciously or unconsciously. Because they are not afraid of it, it does not control them, and they can find appropriate ways of coexistence with it (which include removing it from the places where it is healthier not to have it around). Because they neither deny, fear, nor hate it, they have no need to deny, fear, or hate those who unavoidably display it. And because they have an understanding of themselves as created, not creator, as mortal, earthy, tied up with other people and other species, fragile, funny, and slightly ridiculous, they have no need to despise themselves for the dirtiness of their existence, nor to feel themselves above dealing with it. Instead, like Jesus, getting down on his knees to wash the feet of his friends above their scandalized protests, or Gandhi, taking on the untouchable task of cleaning out the latrines.

Humble, earthy people are therefore not condemned to harshness. Humble people are free to be gentle with those who struggle in the mess and mire of life. It is a strange linguistic confusion that 'gentle' is so often the word used in association with 'humble'. One might say that gentleness is the activity that is the fruit of the spirit of earthiness, because 'gentle' in its original meaning implied exactly the opposite from humble, low-born. It meant well-born (literally, having the right to bear arms), and was used to describe those of high station, gentlefolk, all that was not base. It seems so unlikely a conjunction that we tend to assume that it is another meaning of gentle that is intended, that of being mild-mannered and kind—which again has a distinctly feminine overtone, as in 'the gentler sex'. But perhaps that is not right. Perhaps it *is* gentle in its original sense that is most appropriate. To be gently born has traditionally meant to be honourable, generous, courteous (the 'very gentil, parfait knight' of the *Canterbury Tales* springs to mind). Perhaps what is implied is that there is nothing that could be more honourable than to be born of the earth, of creation, of nature. The 'gentil knight' is one with 'nature's gentleman (and woman)'.

This honourable earthiness is very far from the sanitized sterile virtue that often seems rigid, unrelaxed, dead from the neck down, that seeks desperately to control and banish all that is untidy, unresolved, imperfect. It is equally far from the driving harshness that turns good mud sour with the poison of self- or other-abuse. There is a beautiful and rarely used word whose meaning, to hold dear, is the exact opposite of harshness. It is the word 'cherish'. Cherishing assumes courtesy and respect not based on rank or status, but on equal createdness. It assumes an honour that confers the dignity of intrinsic being on everyone and everything. It assumes generosity in giving and receiving, not just in the heroic, dramatic, or highly visible things that we often want to give and receive, but in the mundane and tedious and intimate things that we are in fact more often called upon to give and receive. Receiving especially, and often more demandingly, because there is a humility in not always needing to be the giver, in offering to others the poss-ibility of equality in a relationship. When Jesus washed feet, it was an act of cherishing, requiring humility and gentleness in both the ones who were washed and the one who washed.

We do not need to seek out opportunities to wash feet today. Every bedbath given, every nappy changed, every body served or tended is a washing of feet. Not done as an opportunity for mortification or spiritual self-abasement (when it is in reality the manifestation of pride or self-loathing), but a conferring of dignity to and from one another:

> From you I receive, to you I give
> Together we learn, and so we live.

BEING AT HOME

The effect of being cherished is to make us feel 'at home'. That is to say, we experience a feeling of at-home-ness that does not depend on being in a certain place or with certain people, but is an experience of welcome, strengthening, acceptance, care. There are people with whom one can feel at-home-ness in a park.

The desire for 'at-home-ness' is a demonstration of spirituality, a deep yearning, the expression of pro-found motivation. A lighted window in a darkened house, a fire kindled, a bowl of flowers on a table, clean sheets, are all powerful symbols of the longing of the human spirit for at-home-ness, for sanctuary, for a place of safety, of cherishing, a strong place, a place that reaches out generously to embrace us when we are weary and battered. Never mind that the lighted window shines from a dreary building, never mind that the fire warms a room decorated with wallpaper from the ends of four different rolls, never mind that the flowers are plastic or the sheets threadbare. At-home-ness does not depend on a definition of good taste gleaned from the pages of *Homes and Gardens*, and sanctuary is not built on the martyrdom of necessity, but on the joy of sufficiency, even the sufficiency of dreams.

These characteristics of cherishing, at-home-ness, earthiness as expressions of humility, need to be clearly differentiated from the unhealthy kind of understanding of humility that characterizes it as a kind of abasement. I call it 'saying thank you for the privilege of being a doormat'. *No one* should ever feel that humility means that, but Christian hagiography is full of it, and there are countless people today, mostly women, but some men too, who have somehow learned from the Church that it's their humble duty to be walked on, have internalized such a negative picture of themselves that they painfully put up with manipulative, abusive, and violent parents, partners, children, or colleagues. Let there be no mistake, this is nothing whatsoever to do with the Christian virtue of humility. It has to do with the abuse of power, and it is never loving, either of oneself or of another, to allow that kind of behaviour to be inflicted on one.

And though an earthy, cherishing spirituality may find women more at ease with it, men too can be (and often are) makers as well as partakers of it. If we all cannot be makers as well as partakers, then there will be nothing left for us to partake of. What we seek to possess, we will end up destroying. An earthy spirituality is the appropriate one for our home the earth. The gentle and humble, those who cherish, those who are 'at home', are the true heirs, those who will inherit the earth. They will not destroy it in their fear of it, nor in the lust for possession, but will possess it in loving it.

The lover of life holds life in his hand,
Like a ring for the bride.
The lover of life is free of dread;
The lover of life holds life in his hand,
As the hills hold the day.

But lust after life waves life like a brand,
For an ensign of pride.
The lust after life is life half-dead;
Yea, lust after life hugs life like a brand,
Dreading air and the ray.

For the sake of life,
For that life is dear,
The lust after life
Clings to it fast.
For the sake of life,
For that life is fair,
The lover of life
Flings it broadcast.

The lover of life knows his labour divine,
And therein is at peace.
The lust after life craves a touch and a sign
That the life shall increase.

The lust after life in the chills of its lust
Claims a passport of death.
The lover of life sees the flame in our dust
And a gift in our breath.

George Meredith

4

A HISTORY NOT PART
OF 'HISTORY'

*Blessed Are Those Who Hunger and Thirst
to See Right Prevail:
They Shall Be Satisfied*

⁂

There is one group of people I know who have been
coming to Iona to spend a week or two there each
year for quite a long time. When I first met them in
the Abbey, it was a pleasure getting to know them,
because they were friendly, open, and knew how to
have a good time. The staff all looked forward to them
coming; someone would say, 'It's the group from Fallin
next week', and everyone would relax, would know that
it was a week to look forward to. We knew that they
would join in the life of the community with enthu-
siasm, would take part in discussion with honesty and
insight, would sing at the ceilidhs unselfconsciously and,
most of all, *they would do their chores*. Whatever else was
going on, however intense the discussion, however beautiful the weather, however enticing the common-room
fire, they would always be there, paying due attention
to this most important function of community life.

And people liked them because they were interested in us, would take us as they found us, would have
no expectations of our being a perfect community.
And they wouldn't expect us to solve their problems.
They were accustomed to dealing with their own

problems. A week with them was like having a week's holiday!

They came from a mining community in Stirlingshire, a typical Scottish mining town, small, grey, close-knit. Most of the men worked in the pits, or had done, and all the others, whatever their jobs, were part of that mining culture. They lived, too, with all the difficulties of mining life—the harsh conditions, the dirt, the terrible insecurity of jobs that has blighted mining in this country for decades. But it didn't make them hard or self-interested. On the contrary, they were among the warmest, wisest, and most caring people I've ever met.

When the miners' strike came in the early 1980s, their colliery, Polmaise, was the first pit out and the last pit back in the whole country. This bitter and protracted dispute, which in so many ways constituted a wholesale assault on some of the finest working people in this country, touched their small community deeply. As well as the political struggle, there was the basic struggle for survival on next to no money. It was a struggle that required a communal response, and that's what it got, as people shared all that they had, opened their homes and their hearts and their pockets. It wasn't just the men. Miners' wives ran soup kitchens, marched for their men, had to become politicized in a new way. At a time when the news was full of images of resistance, conflict, and anger, the mining communities of Scotland—and, I guess, of Britain—were engaged in a remarkable, and perhaps unprecedented, display of solidarity, compassion, and practical care.

My friends belonged to the local church, were faithful members, elders, leaders of organizations. At a time when deep questions of livelihood, identity, justice, and self-worth were being activated, at a time when a gospel paradigm of care was being displayed, in a place where every home in the village was being affected, the local minister did not *once* refer to any aspect of the strike in either preaching or prayer. The people of this community were left to struggle with almost unendurable truths bereft of any word of wholeness from this official representative of the gospel. What saved them were the small ceremonies of grace that came in the soup kitchens and the homes of the mostly unchurched.

I was so angry when I heard that story. Perhaps that's because I felt personally connected with the miners' struggle. My mother's father was a miner, in East Lothian. He died, at the beginning of the 1930s, of one of the miners' diseases, leaving my grandmother, then a woman in her thirties, with seven children, five of them under the age of six, to bring up on her own. Her life too was one of struggle in these days before the Welfare State: of going out to work as a cleaner, of poverty, and hardship and exhaustion. She died in her early fifties when her youngest child was eighteen, her task accomplished—worn out, one supposes. I know that my own life has in subtle ways been shaped by that history, and by some of the injustices implicit in it. It's salutary to remember that single working mothers are by no means a new phenomenon.

And I was born, and spent the first few years of my life, in another mining community—or, at least, a former one—in Dumfriesshire, a ghost town full of memories, empty of work. Perhaps in these vital early years I inherited more of that sense of connectedness, of being in some way tied up with this way of life.

But I think I am in no way unusual. The map of Scotland is marked, from East to West, from North to South, with the traces of mining. It was a huge part of Scottish life, with something like one in five Scots having mining in their blood. That's a million people! It runs very deep in our culture, from Fife to the Lothians, from Ayrshire to Dumfriesshire to Perthshire, and all points in between.

Not just our exterior, but our interior landscape also is dotted with pit bings, rows of miners' cottages, small grey towns, and mothballed machinery. Even though we no longer have a mining industry, we have a history that lives in us right up to the present day—of the slavery of Ayrshire miners, of pit disasters, of struggles for union recognition and safer working conditions, of the three-day week and, most of all, of the miners' strike. Perhaps one of the reasons that Margaret Thatcher was so disliked by so many people in Scotland is our sense that she was the architect of the mortal wounding of part of our soul.

But my sharing of my friends' sense of betrayal is not simply about the mining industry. It is part of a much bigger struggle to confront issues of justice, as a Christian, as a human being. I grew up during the sixties, when all you needed was love. It was a good time to be young, better, it seems to me, than today, a time when you could be hopeful and optimistic, when you could still be innocent about the world, a time when jobs and peace and life seemed to be there just for the taking. Today, innocence goes early, children learn young that you don't talk to strangers, that you have to compete to get the good jobs or, indeed, any job at all, that life is a cruel struggle for survival against drugs and AIDS and the dole. Back in the days of Camelot, it seemed as if it was only a matter of time until we should overcome. Unfortunately, these feelings of benevolence proved to be inadequate to deal with a world whose reality did not quite match the perceptions of the gilded youth of growth economies. The era of love and peace slipped or was torn away in the wake of Vietnam and Watergate, of fallen heroes and Cruise missiles, and we lost our innocence. We all wanted love and peace, but justice, without which there is no peace—ah, that was another thing.

NOT ABSTRACTIONS BUT NECESSITY

I have the sense that justice has moved slightly off the public agenda at the moment. It's not the most popular word in political circles, though slightly more acceptable when prefixed by the word 'social'—a term I find somewhat confusing, for what other kind is there? In an incoherent way, it all seems to be tied up with the demise of communism, the shifting of the political consensus in Britain, a kind of awful helplessness about 'what to do about Africa', and the catastrophic injustices it suffers, reaction against liberation movements, and a general sense of hopelessness about justice ever being achievable.

And yet this fatalism, this sense of doom and helplessness, is continually being confronted. We cannot give up on justice quietly, with a clear conscience. The existential questions it poses remain in human consciousness, even if only at a subliminal level, and, if unexamined, manifest themselves in anxiety, rootlessness, and alienation, leading to an ever-greater defensive hunger for having. The fear that questions of justice arouse cannot be easily allayed, when all the time we are being forcibly reminded of the nature of the world we live in—violent, cruel, and remorseless. Every time a bomb goes off, every time we see the images of famine in the Horn of Africa or atrocity in Bosnia, or racism on the streets of Berlin or Los Angeles or London, or sectarian killing in Belfast, there is a terrible sadness. What was on the back burner of consciousness is dragged into our living-rooms, and we are face to face with issues of justice once again.

Thinking about justice is very difficult. Making decisions about it seems even harder. It seems as if even love is easier than justice, because we know where to start there. We can begin where we are, and we have practical ways of expressing love, ranging all the way from the comforting arm for the distressed person through to small daily acts of help and support for those whose suffering is great. But where to begin with justice? How do we make sense of all its conflicting claims that bombard us? Where is the simple direct truth about justice, if indeed there is such a thing?

And yet we know we cannot as Christians, or just as well-intentioned human beings, deny its claims upon us. Biblical Christianity is rooted in justice; the whole concept of righteousness, right relationship, begins with justice, with equal rights, opening out into an explosion of generosity, of bias to those whom the scales are weighted against, of salvific liberation. Without the starting point of justice as the basis for right relationship, the incarnation, the good news of Jesus Christ, is meaningless.

One of the ways in which I think Western society is in deep difficulty in its understanding of justice is to do with the way in which we approach it, the framework in which it is presented to us. Western political thinking and orthodox Western theology (which share some of the same origins) both start from theory, not from experience. Both begin with a theoretical framework of dogma and doctrines, which in social terms offer 'declaratory, non-enforceable rights'. That is to say, they begin with charters, declarations, manifestos, creeds, and statements, which lay down, often in considerable detail, *how things ought to be*. 'Christians ought to love their neighbours', 'Christians should all get on with one another', 'Christians ought not to tell lies', or 'there ought to be universal human suffrage', 'there ought to be enough training places for young people between the ages of sixteen and eighteen', 'no one should have to wait more than three months for an operation', 'everyone has the right to life, liberty and the pursuit of happiness'. Furthermore, these theoretical frameworks start from a particular standpoint, usually that of power and dominance. They take for granted Western democracies with their dominant economic powers. Or, they begin with the teaching of the Bible or the Church, and the theories are required to ensure that people conform their lives to these. Broadly speaking, they begin from law—and, most often, from law that favours and reinforces the status quo.

But theory is not a good starting point for people who hunger and thirst to see right prevail. People who hunger and thirst are driven by necessity, not abstractions. People who walk hundreds of miles in burning heat don't do it for the sake of the universal declaration of human rights. They do it to feed their children. People who marched in Soweto and Manila and Peking didn't do it for the Ten Commandments or the Thoughts of Chairman Mao or even the Sermon on the Mount. They did it for the freedom to move about their own country, to be paid according to their work and not the colour of their skin, to get out from under the weight of poverty and oppression. People who resist hospital opting-out don't do it for the Citizens' Charter, they do it so that they won't have to apply for their own jobs at hourly rates below £2 an hour. People hunger and thirst for justice so that they may not be utterly dependent on the charity or the cruelty or the whim of others, so that they may have the dignity of being responsible for their own lives, to resist squalor, ugliness, want, homelessness, the definition of their lives as having no intrinsic value or worth, but only that given to it by others (whatever that may be). People hunger and thirst for justice in order that they may be the subjects and not the objects of their own lives.

For people who hunger and thirst for justice, because they experience the lack of it, theory does not and cannot deliver of itself. Justice is never handed down from on high, because it is not in the interest of those on high to deliver it. It has to be struggled for. Justice as promise and not as threat, as hope and not as fear, as possibility and not as problem, can *only* be understood by those who are engaged in struggling for it, by those on the underside of history, by those for whom it represents food and drink, dignity and freedom, choice and responsibility.

Liberation theology has sprung from the experience of those deeply immersed in a liberation struggle to be the subject and not the object of their own existence, who have decided for self-definition and against allowing others to decide who and what and how they will be. It is directed against the structures of those systems that oppress and dehumanize. It begins with people's real-life experience and interprets both Scripture and tradition in the light of that. It is therefore a dynamic theology, a theology of movement and change, not static or once and for all. As such, liberation theologies offer a radical challenge to orthodox theology and political theories. They dethrone as normative, as the definition of what it means to be fully human, white, Western, male experience. On a global scale, it is the struggle to reinterpret history from the underside.

In the Middle Ages, history from the centre, from the throne, said: Europe is Christendom—everyone outside is heathen and needs to be saved. Then it said: Europe is the place of the Enlightenment—everyone outside is savage and needs to be civilized. Finally it said: the West is developed—everyone outside is underdeveloped and needs progress.

The rest of the world has consistently been defined in terms of lack, deficiency, failure, inferiority, and treated accordingly. Mostly this treatment has come in the form of power, control, exploitation, colonialism, and neo-colonialism. Sometimes it has come in the form of 'charity', usually with strings attached. 'Having been made inhuman by the cruel, they are required to be less than human by the kind.' (Howard Barker). People's own self-understanding, their own subjectivity, their own maps, have been ignored, denied, and insulted.

But there have been many groups, many experiences, struggling this century to reinterpret history from the underside. From this struggle have come many liberation theologies: black theology, feminist theology, Latin-American liberation theology, Asian and Minjung theology, gay theology, all struggling under a weight of being imprisoned by theoretical definitions of *what they ought to be* imposed by others, and not expressing the *reality of their experience*.

Perhaps the minister of my mining friends was caught on the horns of a dilemma. His theological training would have given him the theoretical framework that says things like, 'Christians ought not to strike', 'politics should not be mentioned in church' and 'our masters should act with justice'. But, faced with the reality that life was not in fact conforming to theory, that his doctrines and dogmas left him inadequately equipped to deal with ambiguity, conflict, people not acting in the way they were supposed to, being unpredictably right *and* unpredictably wrong (according to theory), perhaps he simply did not know what to say. If he had been able to admit that, confess his confusion, share his doubts, then I think his people, his flock of whom he was supposed to be the shepherd, the pastor, would have understood, sympathized, shared their own doubts and confusion. They would have struggled together, and he would have found the words (or the silences) he needed out of that struggle. But his silence was one of disengagement, of detachment, of power from on high, of the ability to choose to say nothing. And so he became redundant to their lives.

Unless he was quite dead to all pastoral responsibility, I

imagine that his silence caused him anxiety, distress, even fear. It is the way that the powerful are rendered powerless by their own power. Wrong relationship is wrong on both sides, hurts everyone who participates in it.

THE STRUGGLE TO LIVE AS SUBJECT

I am acutely reminded of that fact every time I am with another group who are blessed because they hunger and thirst to see right prevail. I don't know that these are the words they would use to describe what they are about, but they are clear about their struggle for justice. They are part of a group called ATD Fourth World, a movement started by a French Catholic priest called Joseph Wresinski. ATD stands for Aide à Toute Détresse, and the movement seeks to unite all sections of society around its very poorest citizens. The group that I meet with in Glasgow are very poor people, among the poorest in our country. Most of them are unskilled, unemployed, struggling to survive on benefit in bad housing, often on squalid estates, and subject to all the difficulties that accompany poverty—physical illness, mental health problems, family breakdown, drug abuse, lack of opportunity, and a very low opinion of themselves. They are hugely vulnerable to 'the grindings of life and the indifference of men'. By the standards by which our society tends to judge these things, they would not be deemed to have made a success of their lives. Each day is a struggle for survival, and the margins between coping and not coping are acutely narrow.

But I have defined them in terms of what they lack, of deficiency, and I would prefer to describe them in terms of sufficiency, what they possess. I would like you to understand their shattering honesty and openness. I would like you to understand their amazing generosity with what little they have. I would like to communicate to you their humour and resourcefulness, the way they make their hurt work for the good of other people in friendship, encouragement, and mutual help. I would like to communicate their pleasure in small things, things that have become stale and taken for granted by so many of us. I would like you to be able to honour, as I cannot help but do, moments of gruff and profound tenderness as they accompany one another through pain. I would like you to be able to share their creativity, which, in spite of every weight and burden laid upon them, springs irrepressibly through Kay's poetry, Willie's garden, Celia's singing, and all the rest. I would like to share the history that is not part of History.

I wrote a poem for Celia:

> *Rejoicing in Heaven*
>
> She sings like a raucous angel
> —Blessed Patsy Cline of Pollokshields—
> and heaven applauds.
> Earth, on the other hand,
> whose taste is in its arse,
> has not been so appreciative,
> and has rewarded her with
> abusive men,
> crummy houses,
> rotten jobs
> and a tendency to badmouth her
> when she drinks too much.
> However, I have it on good authority
> that when Celia sings
> saints start swaying their hips
> and archangels go all dreamy.
> They like a bit of attitude in heaven.

But nothing I write could communicate her spirit and courage.

What this group does, for itself and with the solidarity of the remarkable loving women who work with them in small, sometimes infinitesimal, ways, is engage in a process, a struggle. That process begins with seeing and naming the chains that bind, not just the external injustices, but the internalized oppression, the way people have taken on the identity given to them by the dominant power ('failure', 'worthless', 'redundant', 'underclass', all using the criteria for success of the dominant power), have conformed to their own objectification. That this internalized oppression is hugely powerful is well known, for example, to those who work with battered women, while others, not seeing these inner chains, are inclined to ask incredulously, 'Why doesn't she just leave him?'

The next part of the process is to do with claiming self-definition, with refusing received identity and putting on one's own authority. You notice that I say claiming self-definition, not claiming the right to it—there's a subtle difference. It's about doing it, not asking permission to do it. This often requires withdrawing from the dominant power and finding one's own space. It's important for the ATD group that they have a flat where they can meet, cook, store goods for their second-hand shop, and so on. It's not wonderful, but it's theirs. This withdrawal was part of the raison d'être of the black consciousness movement in South Africa, of women's groups all over the world, of the conscientization processes of base communities in Latin-America. Often this withdrawal has been a cause of some indignation to liberal, white Western males, including those in the Church, who have not properly understood its necessity, or who have wanted to be politically correct without the pain of the struggle for a new self-definition that does not depend on being the standard by which everyone else is measured. 'I thank God that you did not make me a Gentile or a woman.'

In this set-apart space, the ATD group can begin to be

themselves, freed of the necessity to meet someone else's expectations. They can support one another in doing this. Because it *is* a struggle. It's a struggle to live as subject in the midst of huge objectification and dispensability. It's a struggle to resist being the object of services provided, development delivered, privileges extended, rights defined, and the promise of justice, one day, if you're patient, when the trickle-down theory finally trickles down enough. Not to be grateful for these things invites enormous hostility. And it's also about discovering that identity is never static; it's always dynamic, always in process.

But the great insight of liberation theology, of the hunger and thirst to see right prevail, is that this is not just a concern for justice inspired by a profound motivation of love and anger. It is that, in the interface where vision and motivation meet and engage, *the struggle itself is liberative*. Means and ends are inseparable.

The American philosopher Noam Chomsky argues that, without a system of formal constraints, there are no creative acts, there is only change. Reading about cosmology recently, I came across this development of Chomsky's argument: 'In the tension, at all levels, between the drive for differentiation and the drive for undivided wholeness, there would intuitively seem to be possibilities for the experience of constraint which shapes change into creativity.' The writer here was talking from an ecological perspective, and it certainly appears to me that not only human beings, but the earth itself, is hungering and thirsting for justice, seeking to shake off the chains that bind it. Metaphorically, one could say that it is a description of how the earth is struggling to free itself from its oppressive burdens, how it's fighting back. Earth resists the cutting-down of rain forests and soil erosion with water. But creativity is not necessarily good from all points of view, and there are people in the way of the floods.

Certainly, though, it is a description of the effects of liberation struggles. It is not just that the goal is justice, is liberation. It is that, in the struggle, creative action is liberated. In struggling to satisfy the hunger and thirst for right relationships, the hunger and thirst actually begins to be satisfied, in so far as the means themselves are those of justice, of right relations. This is my understanding of the blessedness Jesus referred to. It is what I saw and shared in the community both of my mining friends, and of the ATD group.

If we can only know this blessedness if we stand with the underside of history, the history that is not part of History, and if we are actively engaged in the struggle for justice, then I think that poses particular problems for our society with its culture of economic and spiritual capitalism. A struggle, by definition, requires limitations, restrictions, confines against which to push. I want to tell a number of stories that I believe illustrate the problems.

❦ · ❦

THE FLIGHT FROM FINITENESS

Last summer, I was in John O'Groats waiting for a ferry to Orkney. In the Visitor Centre there, is a beautifully presented exhibition illustrating the history of Caithness from Neolithic times. I carefully read every word on the large boards, and realized with amazement that there was no mention whatsoever of the Highland Clearances, nor of the famines and land struggles of the nineteenth century. This is a county that suffered greatly, where a whole culture and way of life was eroded. The exhibition did not of itself surprise me. What depressed me was that the people of Caithness allowed their history to be distorted

71

in such a way. This is not just a denial of people's past, it is their present also. Today, the whole of the huge county of Caithness is in the legal possession of less than twenty people or companies.

This story is repeated all over Scotland: in the history of our own country that is omitted in school; in the repression of memories of bad working conditions and the squalor of industrial slums, which are beginning to reappear in a new way; in the offer of 900 words in the *Dictionary of Scottish Church History and Theology* to assess the contribution of women in the Church of Scotland over two millennia. But it is not just the story of the hurts done to us, and their continuing consequences, that is denied and repressed. It's also the hurts done by Scots to others. Unless we remember where we have been not only victims but also perpetrators of injustice, our struggles for justice will lead us into arrogance—and injustice. To redeem our history, we must remember it, with its offences as well as its wounds. *Both personally and politically, our society encourages us to disengage from the confines and demands and limitations of our history.*

Every day after collecting my daughter from school, we stand at a pedestrian crossing at one of the busiest corners of one of Glasgow's busiest roads. And every day I see drivers jump the lights, stop within inches of toddlers, sit on the crossing, or even drive right across it when the lights are red. I am staggered that decent people, who would be horrified if you gave them a gun and told them to go out and kill a pensioner or a six-year-old, will dice with human life in order to save ninety seconds. And I wonder what they are going to do with the ninety seconds. We know about the carnage on the roads, and about the ecological threat of the car. But we go on with the madness anyway. *Both personally and politically, our society encourages us to disengage from the confines and demands and limitations of our geography.*

❧❦ · ❧❦

A friend told me recently of a woman who said despairingly, 'My life would improve dramatically if someone would just kill Joe.' Joe is her husband. Every day he sits on the sofa watching TV and, because he can't be bothered to get up, he pisses on the sofa. Every night his wife sleeps on the same sofa because he won't let her sleep in the bed. Of course, he's not a happy man. He's unemployed, he's poor, and because he feels life has pissed on him, he pisses on his wife. He could join her in struggling to survive with some dignity. But is he too weak? Might he become stronger by struggling? He gets such confused messages from society. An extreme story? Of course!
Both personally and politically, our society encourages us to disengage from the confines and demands and limitations of interrelatedness.

❧❦ · ❧❦

A princess starves and vomits. Women have plastic surgery to maintain the illusion of youth. We have a social culture that denies the giftedness of ageing, a sexual culture that degrades and armours and hurts bodies because it cannot value diversity.
Both personally and politically, our society encourages us to disengage from the confines and demands and limitations of bodies.

❧❦ · ❧❦

Our language and symbols speak eloquently. An end to

history. The world's your oyster. No such thing as society. The right to economic growth. The need to stimulate consumerism. Retail therapy. We live in a society that entices with limitlessness, that offers escape from the demands of finiteness.

Reality, of course, is something different. The reality is that we live finite lives on a finite planet. Rolling back the boundaries simply means that they roll over someone else. Our unlimited freedom is someone else's prison, someone else's injustice. The costs don't go away. They get externalized on to someone else—the poor, women, other cultures, the earth. We extol the cross. We just want someone else to carry it.

There are particular difficulties about this kind of material and spiritual accumulation. There is the difficulty of differentiation between the misery of libertarianism and the pain of injustice. We have plenty of liberty, but not a lot of liberation. There is the problem that if we inhabit a construct in which everything is possible, everything has its theoretical justification, there is never the profound relief and release of repentance and confession and forgiveness. And because we operate outwith the confines of history and geography and interrelatedness and bodies, we can always avoid being confronted with the concreteness of *this place and this time*. Justice becomes located in a mythical past or a theoretical future: 'in the good old days', 'Victorian values', 'when I've solved my problems', 'when the economy improves'. So we tolerate the 'obscenity of the now', and wonder why people are not more grateful. We hail the makers of concessions as great champions of human rights. And, if all else fails, there is always the age-old remedy of blaming the victim.

If I understand correctly, liberation, justice, righteousness, are not goals on some far-distant horizon. Nor are they freedom from limitations. Rather, they are the recognition, first, of the reality, the God-givenness, the intrinsic potential of all creation and of every person to be the subject and not the object of her or his own life. And second, they are engagement (within the confines of a concrete, historical, geographical, embodied present) in the struggle to resist and remove all that denies or degrades or distorts that reality, and to seek the society that embraces it. And third, they are the joyful and hopeful fruit of that engagement, which, in my small experience, is far sweeter than the enticing but tasteless fruit of the spiritual free market. This is the paradox known to artists and poets: that it is in struggling not to deny, the tightest form, but instead to transform it, that the greatest creative freedom is liberated. This creative freedom I see incarnated in my friends from the mining community, and in the Glasgow ATD group.

I used to go on Reclaim the Night marches. These were a response by women to the lack of freedom and safety to walk the streets at night. The fear of assault, attack, and rape is strong for women, but these women had got fed up with policemen and others telling them to stay indoors at night or, if they had to go out, only to go in groups, and to certain places. This is called making the victim bear the cost, and it simply increases fear and vulnerability. Many women still do that without even thinking about it. They haven't yet seen their chains. Others have adopted what might be called the Western theological model. They go to self-defence classes, and avail themselves of the right to react in terms dictated by the threatening power. Still others simply avoid the restriction by driving everywhere, an option open only to the minority. But the marches were about taking back what is the potential of *everyone*. We invited people to join us, and some did. We requested others—some who jeered or abused us—that if they couldn't join us, then not to hinder us, to please get out of the way. For a brief moment of freedom to walk the streets of our own city at night unafraid, we knew the blessedness of that desire, that hunger and thirst, fully satisfied.

5

STRONG AT THE BROKEN PLACES

Blessed Are the Merciful:
God Will Be Merciful to Them

﷽

Cathy is one of those people who can brighten up the darkest day. Every now and then I meet her, getting on the Underground, coming out of work, or in the shopping centre, and we stop and chat, exchange news of our children and our churches, wish each other well, and go our separate ways—me always with my spirit lifted by closeness to her warmth and gaiety. But I will always remember one time when we shared a week together in Iona Abbey, and I saw her work a little miracle.

Cathy lives in an inner-city, working-class neighbourhood of Glasgow, and works in a children's daycare centre. She's a very attractive woman of about fifty, I supoose, though she looks younger: auburn-haired, trim, and always well turned out. But it's the warmth and vitality and zest for life that she radiates that is the most attractive thing about her. She's been divorced for a long time, and has raised her three daughters more or less single-handed. I don't imagine life has been particularly easy for her; she must have had her share, and perhaps more than her share, of hurt, worry, and hard work. But I don't know her history—she's much more inclined to talk cheerfully about the positive things in her life, or share her present struggles, than dwell on the pain of the past.

She has also been involved in her local church, and it was with a small group from that church that she came to Iona Abbey to spend a week in a quieter time of the year. As well as the group from her church, there was another group staying in the Abbey—also from Glasgow, but very different from the grannies, weans, and respectable Christians in the church group. This was a group of recovering alcoholics from a hostel in Glasgow, a place that often brought men up to Iona at quiet times of the year, where they could enjoy the peace and beauty of the island, relax around a different fireside of an evening, and share in the friendship and acceptance of the community life.

Almost all of these men were deeply hurt and broken people. They came trailing broken marriages, lost jobs, soured friendships, neglected responsibilities. They carried the knowledge of degradation, violence, and sometimes crime. Each of them, no matter what their background or age (and they were various), hauled chains of memory, guilt, failure, and fear around with them. In particular, guilt about their treatment of women—wives, mothers, daughters—had left them with a pervasive sense of failure as men—as husbands, sons, fathers. They had lost confidence in any value to their manhood. These men were vulnerable, fragile, defeated. And the fact that they had inflicted grievous wounds on others, often the people they cared about most, did not make them any less hurt.

Their vulnerability meant that at first they were very insecure in a strange environment. While the church group chatted happily with members of staff and volunteers, made friends with strangers at the meal table, and joined in every new activity—from communal dishwashing to daily worship—with gusto, the men clung together. They stayed close to the common-room fireside, sat together at meals (and looked panicky if there was not a seat available for them), and ventured out for walks in twos and threes. In church, they were tentative. They would come in at the last minute, sit in the row furthest back, and listen intently without joining in.

So for the first few days, they were a tight group within a much larger, more fluid, community. Members of staff made initial approaches, then had to go off to do their work. Children played round them, and the men themselves watched like children observing a game going on from the edge—eager to be asked, ready to return a stray ball, but fearful of pushing in unasked for fear of rejection.

But one person set out from the beginning of the week to bridge the gap. At the very first meal, Cathy set herself down in the middle of a table of the men, and at almost every meal thereafter she was to be found surrounded by them, quite undaunted, smiling, joking, talking animatedly. During choretime she marshalled her little band of men with buckets and mops dangling awkwardly from their hands, with a combination of generalship and intuition, encouraging them—as if to say, 'OK, lads, I know this is woman's work, and you feel doubtful enough about your role without being given a mop and bucket, but I'm the expert here, and it's all right to go along with it, I won't think any the less of you because of it.' In the evenings she sat with them till late into the night, drinking coffee, talking, listening, reassuring, laughing, and most of all accepting.

And because she was a pretty woman, vivacious and flirtatious and humorous, they began to respond like men. They began to unwind, to relax, to stand a little taller, to speak with a little more confidence. They each began to be a little more distinctive; a little more different; marked not by their similarities of diffidence, but by individual characteristics. One emerged as the joker, another as the thinker, another as the practical handyman. They began to speak of their past in a different way, not of their failures but of their accomplishments, of skills they had, places they'd been, tasks they'd taken pride in. And as they relaxed in themselves, they began to relax with other people as well. They began to mix at the mealtable, to join in the children's games, to move in from the back in the church.

On the last night, there was a dance in the village hall. All week, Cathy had been teasing the men about going to it, about which dances they were going to give her, and all week they had been refusing even to countenance the suggestion. But that Friday night, we all went to the dance—the weans, the grannies, the staff, the men, and Cathy. She danced with every one of them. And that night, I think they all fell a little in love with her. Everyone had a good time, and as we came home there was more noise than there had any right to be at 1 a.m. on a quiet Hebridean island.

As I said, it was like watching a little miracle unfolding. Others might have come along and tried to be good Christians in the situation. They might have talked and listened sympathetically, commiserated with these men in their difficulties, withheld judgement on their failures. They might have done their very best to approach them as fellow human beings at a low ebb, in need of support and understanding. And the miracle would not have happened. Because still, however kindly, the focus would have been on their problems and not their potential, on their impotence and not their potency. What Cathy did was to treat them as *men*, and invite them, ever so gently and without threat, to rise to that challenge—and they did. She gave them back a little pride.

Cathy might have been one of their wives. She had certainly been deeply hurt in the most intimate of relationships between men and women. It would have been easy for her to let her own pain close herself off from feeling for theirs, to be wary of taking the risk of relationship, particularly with men who were not reliable or stable—and had been proven to be anything but. She

80

might have chosen to ignore them, to patronize them, to humiliate them. But she didn't. Whatever her own history and hurt, she acted out of something different. She was merciful.

❧ · ❧

FALLING IN LOVE AGAIN

Eight years ago, I fell in love with mercy. Mercy is not a person. Mercy, that quality described by Portia in the *Merchant of Venice* as 'not strained'. Does that seem a strange thing to do, to fall in love with a quality? Maybe it is, but I can find no better way to describe the excitement, recognition, and delight—and also the pain, terror, and sense of destiny—that have pursued me ever since in my unfolding relationship with mercy. Let me try to explain something of what I mean.

In Iona Abbey that summer we were following a programme based on the Beatitudes, and had been preaching on each of them in turn every Sunday. It fell to me to deliver a sermon on 'Blessed Are the Merciful'. My mind was somewhat blank when approaching the task. It was not one of the Beatitudes I felt greatly inspired by; it did not move me like some of the others. In fact, I really had rather negative feelings about the whole subject. The word 'mercy' seemed to me the worst kind of religious word, meaningless in most people's experience, a clichéd term trotted out to dress something up in pious language. It seemed to have something to do with forgiveness, but in a patronizing, almost demeaning, way. The truth is that for me, mercy had got stuck in the nineteenth century. Its overtones were quintessentially Victorian, 'little deeds of mercy, little acts of toil', angels of mercy in white caps, a soft hand on a fevered brow and the shadow of a lamp on a wall. It was, or it might as well have been, the name

81

of revolting Victorian heroines in improving moral tales. It had, for me, been reduced to the status of religious window-dressing.

Perhaps some of my more unconscious distaste for the word came from associating it with the wettest descriptions of femininity (with which I was greatly out of sympathy, knowing that I could never in a thousand years fit them); that peculiar habit of ascribing to womanhood (at least, to good womanhood) all kinds of wonderful qualities and pure ideals, and then using them to justify keeping women out of the public arena and confining them to a purely domestic sphere. If women were by nature and inclination 'the civilizing influence', 'the gentle touch', 'the upholder of Christian values', 'the angels of mercy', then that put them in a position where they had to be protected from the cut and thrust of public life, shielded from discomfort and dirt, shielded to preserve these feminine qualities in case they were tarnished by association with the harsher side of life. Men, those naturally more boisterous, less refined creatures, were presumably assumed to be less capable of displaying these qualities (or, at least, without seriously threatening received notions as to the nature of what it is to be a 'real man'). Now, at a time when 'Victorian values' are dredged up from time to time as an exemplar, it is interesting to refect on this deep separation, which actually took place in an era whose actual treatment of women below the middle classes (and sometimes included even them) could be brutal verging on inhuman. All this in a period that, perhaps more than any other, claimed to be inspired by Jesus Christ, a man who displayed the kind of humility, powerlessness, and gentleness the Victorians seemed to admire only in some of their women. Be that as it may, 'mercy' had for me become resolutely stuck in the nineteenth century, and removed from the common currency of my life.

In this context, therefore, I sat down to write a sermon

on mercy. But fate intervened, as is sometimes the case when people fall in love. I discovered that my very-much admired Professor of Old Testament was staying on the island. I decided that whatever I wrote, it would be the result of some careful study and reflection. So I hauled out every commentary and dictionary and book I could find, and started to do some work on mercy.

And I experienced what amounted to revelation. (I apologize to those of you who have always known this—I am much less young and self-assured now!) I discovered that *mercy* is one of the great words of the Bible. Both in its subtle range of meaning, and in the extent of its use, it is a word of power. It is a definitive quality of God in both Old and New Testaments. It is essential to the being of God, and occurs hundreds of times both as description and as command. It is the quality of love that the Psalmists ached for and the prophets called for, that Jesus made absolutely human and the disciples struggled with. It is what the Christian Church throughout its history has made the first act of the great salvation drama of worship, so that day by day and week by week Christians of every tradition and in every language sing, chant, pray, and cry *Kyrie Eleison, Lord have mercy on us, Christe Eleison, Christ have mercy on us*. It is freedom, healing, love. It is the word of life.

My Victorian images would have been of little use to the Psalmist writing, 'I am worn out, O Lord, have pity on me, give me strength. I am completely exhausted and my whole being is deeply troubled. Come and save me, Lord, in your mercy, rescue me from death. . . . I am worn out with grief; every night my bed is damp from weeping, my pillow is soaked with tears.' (Ps. 6.2–7, (GNB)). Or to the one who cried in torment, 'My strength is gone, gone like water spilt out on the ground. All my bones are out of joint, my heart is like melted wax, my throat is dry as dust and my tongue sticks to the roof of my mouth.' (Ps. 22.14–15, (GNB)).

83

Every experience of anguish, terror, feebleness, despair, every moment of failure, humiliation, abandonment, weakness that we have ever had is in these cries. They are cries for all times, all conditions, all humanity. They are the cries of extremity, and they demand an extreme response.

The Hebrew word *ḥesed* in the Old Testament, which is most often translated as *mercy*, is in fact a word that is so rich in meaning that we cannot adequately contain it in English. It holds within it qualities of love, faithfulness, kindness, solidarity. It has been expressed in various translations as 'loving kindness', as 'steadfast or constant love'. Other words in the Old and New Testaments seeking to express this quality contain a range of meaning that includes grace, motherliness, compassion, forgiveness.

It was this last, forgiveness, that I—and I imagine others—most commonly associate with the mercy of God. And yet in the Bible, mercy is even greater than forgiveness. It is the whole activity of God in our lives: a forgiveness that does not bind us to living with what we cannot live with, but releases us from bondage to our past; it is a grace that does not look for repayment, but goes on giving generously and lovingly to 'good' and 'bad' alike; it is a healing that accepts us in all our brokenness, and requires only our admission of wound and offence to meet us. And I saw that this great quality of mercy was embodied in Jesus in compassion and solidarity.

Having stumbled upon mercy, I began to think about the activity of mercy and about how it shows up in people's lives. Two of the words used in the Bible to describe its work struck me with great impact. The first is the word 'compassion'. Compassion is more than pity. It is the sympathetic appreciation of the other as person, the ability not merely to concentrate blindly upon them, but, in so far as anyone can enter the experience of another, to feel with them, to look at things from their point of view, to honour their subjectivity, their own experience of themselves. It is to see the enemy as human, at its extremity. And it is not merely to feel, to be sentimental, but to imagine, to respect, to reflect, and to choose.

Compassion is not detached and impersonal. It is involved, burning, passionate. It is not, I think, possible to be compassionate without being passionate also. It is not by chance that Christ's suffering and death are referred to as the Passion. To be passionate is to suffer in its archaic sense of allowing, experiencing—whether that suffering, that allowing, that experiencing, is of love or sorrow, anger, pain, or joy.

Jesus himself repeatedly pointed to people who had experienced much, who had sometimes been greatly wrong in their allowing, as having the greatest potential for love, whose passion could be transformed into compassion by extending its focus to another rather than the self. The prodigal son, the prostitute who anointed Jesus—whoever has been forgiven much shows much love. The language of passionate love is not temperate. There is a verse in 1 John that reads in a modern translation: 'If a rich man sees his brother in need, yet closes his heart against his brother, how can he claim that he loves God?' The same verse is expressed with far greater power in the Authorized Version: 'But whoso hath this world's good, and seeth his brother have need, and shutteth up his bowels of compassion from him, how dwelleth the love of God in him?'(1 John 3.17.) The bowels of compassion—dredged up from the depths of our being for those with whom we may have no intellectual sympathy. This is no Victorian platitude. This is something that will be hardest with those before whom we are most exposed, or in situations in which we feel the least confidence.

And if compassion is the activity of mercy in our personal relationship, then it seemed to me that solidarity is its corporate or political dimension. Mercy is the mark of the redeemed community as well as the changed individual. The Old Testament paints a picture of the utter faithfulness of God to the people of Israel through backsliding and idolatry, injustice and greed, faithfulness to a covenant relationship that loathed and lamented these things, yet never turned away from the possibility of restored relationship.

The solidarity of Jesus raised people to their feet and stood beside them in defying shame, stigma, oppression. Lepers, the poor, women acting out of conformity, children, foreigners, criminals, outcasts; Jesus identified himself with their vulnerability, their powerlessness, and their perceived threat to the powerful, to the extent of sharing their fate.

And turning from the Bible to my world, I saw something of that kind of solidarity being expressed in the campaign against the callous exploitation of women and children by baby-milk companies, called out by the extremely personal compassion felt by women for their sisters who had watched their babies die of malnutrition. And I saw solidarity in the action and prayer of people who worked untiringly, and often at considerable cost, for justice and its fruit of peace in a hundred places of totalitarian tyranny. I saw it in a hundred little action groups, and a thousand campaigns, and everywhere that people, moved by personal compassion, stand together in solidarity against everything that dehumanizes. I began to see the activity of mercy everywhere around me.

And so I discovered and fell in love with mercy, and was captivated by it. Like all great loves, it began with dazzlement at its beauty. Since then, I have seen something more of its true cost. But it is a relationship that will not let me go, and for this I am grateful to that twist of fate whereby we met face to face. The Professor did not come to hear my sermon. But mercy entered my vocabulary, and enriched it beyond measure.

❦ · ❦

THEE AND ME

And nowhere have I found evidence of the activity of mercy, nowhere have I become more aware of both its power and its necessity, than in the area of sexuality. By sexuality, I do not just mean who we have sex with, although that is obviously a part of the whole. I mean all the relationships by which our sexual identity is defined. Thus I include, as well as partners and lovers, our relationships with parents, sisters and brothers, friends, and teachers and colleagues, for in all of these we learn what it means to be a woman or a man.

Perhaps I find the activity of mercy so important in these relationships because of all the Beatitudes it seems the most personal, the most intimate, the most relational. It is the one above all that demands the presence of the other. Other Beatitudes denote absence, or a way of personal presence, to oneself, to God, to life itself. But the merciful, or those who would be merciful, stand face to face with another, or others. And in this otherness we come to know our own selfhood.

And if mercy is most intimate, most relational, so is our sexuality. It is basic to the way we understand ourselves, accept ourselves and know ourselves, and thence to the way we understand, know, and accept others. So it is also basic to our spirituality, for our sexuality shapes and directs some of our profoundest motivation.

87

To enter the spirituality of sexuality is to enter a mine-field. Its history is one of great distortion, not least by the Christian Church, which is only now beginning to throw off centuries of damaging and dishonest hypocrisy. And even now, it is still incredibly difficult for the Church to address issues such as homosexuality, sex outside marriage, sexuality in the context of age or disability, marital breakdown, and many of the other issues people struggle over agonizingly, with honesty, creativity, and mercy. The experience of so many of us is that the Church will not thank us if we ask difficult questions, often out of places of deep pain, will condemn us or humiliate us or ignore us if we find the restatement of where the Church thinks we ought to be simply does not speak to our actual condition, and will more readily forgive us financial profiteering, unjust working practices, or indifference to the plight of suffering neighbours than it will a failed marriage or touching the body of another person in love if that human being is of the same gender. It has taken the pandemic of AIDS, the incredible suffering of people worldwide, and the considerable courage of some people with AIDS in this country to begin to open the Pandora's Box of sexuality and its spirituality, which has remained closed for so long.

It's inevitable that this should be an enormously painful process, loosing some of our most deeply rooted fears and hatreds along with the beginnings of liberation, and the glimmers of a new, more responsible, sexual ethic. It releases the fear of any connection at all between sexuality and spirituality, the fear of the flesh, mortal and earthy as it is. It issues forth with all the signs of carnality, with blood and sweat and semen. It releases the fear and threat of physical pleasure. It is tempting and dangerous. And, therefore, much too risky to keep shut up in that Pandora's Box like a pressure cooker threatening to blow its lid off.

Sexuality is a powerful and dynamic force in all of life. Attempts to reduce it to a kind of tame domesticity or a starry-eyed romantic idyll are as naive as they are foolish. It has such an awesome potential to hurt, to degrade, and to destroy; and to do so where the damage is most acutely felt, at the very core of our understanding of ourselves as persons. But sexuality also has an equal potential to heal, to transform, and to empower. Such power and dynamism needs to be approached with respect, with care, with mercy.

Today there is a much greater awareness of the need to affirm diversity of life choices and vocations, to value singleness and community as much as marriage, so that these can truly be freely chosen options. We are now much more likely to see our life choices in the area of sexuality as vocational, that is, what will bring true wellbeing rather than what is prescribed by convention. There is less of the idea that marriage means a kind of second-rate service to God or to others. There is also less of the notion that single people should avoid 'dangerous' friendships and intimacy because that would threaten their single-minded service to God or to others. There is less attempt to make people feel guilty because they have sexual needs and desires, and a greater awareness that sexuality in its broadest sense, as well as in sexual intercourse, may be a gift that enriches us rather than an enemy lying in wait always ready to pounce. All this is very good, and goes far towards repairing the damage of the past. But sexuality is above all relational, and all relationships, whether straight or gay, whether inclusive or exclusive of sexual intercourse, whether married or single, will be exactly as mature as the partners within them.

And so it's important to remember exactly what sex is, and avoid the temptation to be too romantic or pious or casual about it. Sex is first of all about bodies, the bodies of people. We still have a tendency to want to get away from bodies.

Sometimes we do that by covering sexuality with a veneer of romance. Well, indeed, romance has its own elements of delight. But sex is about bodies, the possibility of pregnancy and sexually transmitted diseases, bedsharing, and an intimacy that is shattering to all our illusions about the beloved. Something that is entered into as reality rather than simply as the trappings of reality is positively dangerous, when the actual reality becomes much too much to cope with. How many people escape from an unsatisfactory relationship into a fantasy of 'if only' and thus avoid the necessity of dealing with the real relationship they have on their hands. There are no ideal marriages, there are only imperfect ones. But there are better and worse ways of engaging with reality. It is a brutal and necessary rebuttal of the illusion of romance to remember that arranged marriages have just as much chance of success as romantic ones (and even contain within them the possibility of delight).

And sometimes we try to get away from bodies by a fixation with them. We cover our sexuality with a veneer of sexiness. This may seem a strange and contradictory thing to say. But pornography, sexual violence, being macho, are all about a very deep fear of bodies. Pornography is the tool of people who find little delight in their own bodies and their own sexuality, and seek something that is a poor substitute in the bodies of untouchable strangers who have no status as persons for the user, but are a commodity being sold as escape, relief, and the illusion of potency. Casual sex may originate in a genuine desire for intimacy and for an encounter with another that has some meaning, but it takes place in a way that ignores the status of the other as a person with a history, with needs and hopes, with the potential for belovedness. Casual sex blunts the impact that the intimacy of bodies is able to offer, because it does not take the time and care to know the body as a person. Sexual violence is the activity of people who hate their own bodies, may secretly both desire and fear the expression of tenderness, and therefore fear the bodies of other people (usually women). It is not about sex at all, but about power over others in which sexuality becomes nothing more than a weapon. And macho sex is more about lack of confidence in the ability to give and receive pleasure than anything else, leading to a need constantly to put it to the test. All of these are far removed from the place where two people stand naked and defenceless in the presence of each other and are confronted by the mystery of otherness and the possibility of union.

And sometimes we try to get away from our bodies by being religious about them. We cover our sexuality with a veneer of spirituality. We acknowledge that the spiritual can find expression in physical intimacy, but we still have difficulty in seeing the physicality itself as an expression of the spiritual. We always want there to be a reason for sex (being somewhat tied to utilitarianism, perhaps), whether it be for the procreation of children, or to make us love one another more, or to make the family unit stronger, or to give us an experience of the divine nature of marriage or of God. It is almost as if we are saying that the sexuality we enjoy should always serve some greater mystical purpose rather than being enjoyed for its own sake. The metaphor of fruitfulness in sexuality is a beautiful one, and creative sexuality will always bear fruit, but not if that is its main purpose. Trees don't blossom simply in order to get the flowers out of the way so the fruit can come. And it's possible for extremely destructive sex to result in procreation without there ever having been a flowering. We need not be ashamed of the fact that sex is, biologically, an animal act. It's how we were made! Pleasure in sexuality for its own sake is not cause for guilt. We don't feel the need when listening to a beautiful piece of music to insist that by listening we must become better people or have a deeper experience of God or go off and compose a symphony ourselves. The music itself is sufficient reason for listening. The music itself is a gift. So we must be free to know that pleasure *for its own sake* is not naughty or bad. It is as acceptable for the bed to shake as for the earth to move.

Perhaps all this seems a long way from mercy. But all that we understand about our sexuality, and the use we are able to make of it, is very much affected by the ideas we have inherited and by the attitudes of our society. And it is where we are, not where we would like ourselves or our society to be, that mercy is so important to our sexuality. Carrying deep within us, as we do, all the fears, insecurities, and expectations of this so important part of our being, we are inevitably going to experience damage and hurt. No amount of keeping the rules will change that, and indeed may simply exacerbate it. And the extent to which we find healing and wholeness for our wounded sexuality will depend on the extent to which we find mercy—both mercy from others, and mercy from ourselves to ourselves and to others. I understand such mercy to be the expression of God's mercy transmitted through human persons.

It is for the expression of mercy exactly where people were that I so much love one particular story out of that great and merciful book, *Schindler's Ark*, by Thomas Keneally. In a labour camp in the shadow of Auschwitz, a young Jewish couple are conducting a courtship against all the odds:

92

In Rebecca's barracks, the older women took Josef at his word. If Josef required a traditional courtship, they would fall into their traditional role as chaperones. Josef was a gift to them too, a licence to play their pre-war ceremonial selves. From their four-tiered bunks they looked down on the two children until everyone fell asleep. If any one of them thought, Let's not be too fussy in times like these about what the children get up to at dead of night, it was never said. In fact, two of the older women would crowd into the one narrow ledge so that Josef could have a bunk of his own. The discomfort, the smell of the other body, the risk of the migration of lice from your friend to yourself—none of that was as important, as crucial to self-respect, as that the courtship should be fulfilled according to the norms.

And again, after a secret marriage ceremony in the hut:

The couple had been given the top bunk of the tier. For the sake of privacy, it had been hung with blankets. In darkness, Josef and Rebecca climbed to it, and all around them the earthy jokes were running. At weddings in Poland there was always a period of truce where profane love was given its chance to speak. If the wedding guests didn't wish to voice the traditional double entendres themselves, they could get in a professional wedding jester. Women who might, in the twenties and thirties have sat up at weddings making disapproving faces at the risque hired jester and the belly-laughing men, only now and then permitting themselves—as mature women—to be overcome with amusement, stepped tonight into the place of all the absent and dead wedding jesters of southern Poland.

Mercy. The quality that goes, in compassion and solidarity, where in justice it need not!

It is a hard thing to admit, but justice, so crucial in human relationship, is simply not enough in our sexual relationship. We may measure our rights and responsibilities in health, education, employment, political and economic equality, racial and religious and ideological tolerance by the yardstick of justice. We may use justice as the standard by which we determine our relationships with colleagues, with neighbours, with fellow citizens, with other countries. We may pursue justice as the redression of balances for all oppressed and exploited people. And justice may, and should be, a cornerstone of all loving and intimate relationships in their outworking. But there are whole realms of relationship where justice does not run—not even like a little trickle, never mind a mighty river. Where is justice for the man or woman whose capacity for sexual love has never been wanted? Where is justice for the nineteen-year-old girl who is just discovering her sexuality and finds she has only a few months to live? Where is justice for the disabled man who would like to be married but is unable to have sexual intercourse? Where is justice for the homosexual whose sexuality is a source of shame to him, and whose shame is compounded by society's insistence on his deviance? Where is justice for the woman whose husband has left her for a much younger woman? Where is justice for the man who feels despised by his wife because he is not the person she thought she had married? Where is justice for any of us who have ever loved someone who did not love us back, and who therefore have felt ourselves to be a failure? Justice is not enough for any of these. Only mercy offers the possibility of healing.

And once again, I find myself coming back to bodies. If our wounds are bodily, our healing is also bodily. The resurrection of the body is not, I think, simply a spiritual or eternal category. It is also a here and now reality. In a culture that places an overly high value on physical perfection, there is mercy in the action that affirms the gawky adolescent, that creates a climate where everyone

94

can dance, regardless of whether they have a partner or not, that performs basic functions for the sick person with unobtrusive grace, that enters the minefield of the double bed with humour and warmth. At a time when I, who love to dance, was without a partner and felt it as a double hurt, I loved one man who always danced with me, but never in a way that made it feel as if he was doing me a favour because he was sorry for me, but rather made me feel that he was enjoying the dance as much as I was. There is such potential for humiliation and lasting damage in all these areas that they can sometimes only be redeemed by loving kindness. Not the patronizing kind that says, 'There but for the grace of God go I', but the humble kind that says, 'There have I been and there will I be—fat, lonely, impotent, ageing—and entirely lovable.'

※·※

THE SACRAMENTS OF MERCY

There is a beautiful prayer written by a Brazilian, Rubem Alves, which begins thus:

> My God, I need to have signs of your grace.
> Serve me your sacraments,
> the first fruits of your Kingdom.
> I thirst for smiles,
> for sweet odours,
> for soft words,
> for firm gestures,
> for truth and goodness,
> and for triumphs
> (no matter how small)
> of justice.

Mercy is so often communicated in these sacraments,

these healing things. I have a friend who does a lot of work with women's groups, especially with women who have been abused or whose lives are in numerous ways impoverished. Among the activities she does with them are foot massage, aromatherapy, meditation, and relaxation exercises. Her style is characterized by smiles, sweet odours, soft words, and firm gestures. In the midst of lives that have been brutalized, with women who have been conditioned to think of themselves as worthless, of no account, or whose lives have been so taken up with caring for others that there has been no space for themselves, she makes a space. Into that space she introduces new and seductive things—candlelight and scented oils, the sound of silence and of gentle music, respectful listening, and sympathetic touch. It is a sacrament of care, of cherishing, given appropriate and contemporary form. It says clearly, 'You matter, you are worth cherishing, it's all right for you to care for yourself as well as others.'

These are also the kind of sacramental activities that characterize so much of the creative response to HIV and AIDS. If it is indeed true that by their fruits you shall know them, and that where love and mercy are, there is God, then I think it is indeed the case that God is there where our society (and often our Church) least expects and is intentionally blind to—among gays and addicts and accepting relatives and friends. Perhaps we make ourselves blind in order to avoid looking at what we would rather not see in ourselves, and that we prefer to attribute to others.

Or perhaps it is that we can value mercy when it is expressed as individual compassion, but feel uncomfortable when solidarity shows up as the corporate or political dimension of mercy: being resolutely visible and solid; asking embarrassing questions; begging to differ; demanding to be treated as real and not symbolic. Real mercy refuses privatization, requires the same principles to be practised in the public dimension as in the personal. Jesus' teaching is never only personal. It also calls for the transformation of structures and institutions. There is mercy at work in the struggle to extend democratic rights to people in psychiatric institutions and prisons, in the need to challenge in a radical way work patterns that render so many people redundant, in the serious engagement that needs to happen around changing family and community patterns in more than just knee-jerk reaction.

Because all of these things touch every one of us. As we show mercy, so will mercy be shown to us. This is not just a question of thoughts and feelings, of words and talk. 'And some have compassion, making a difference' (Jude 22,AV). Our love must be true love, which shows itself in action.

One of the difficult things about forgiveness, which is so often such a crucial dimension of mercy, is that if it remains theoretical, an intellectual assent, or a laudable sentiment, it is not transformative and remains simply a kind of exercise of will, liable to being blown about, and to building up inner resentment. *It is only action that is transformative, only action that effects actual change—not just in the situation but also in us.* However good our intentions, without action there is stasis.

I have a cousin who lives in Canada. She had a good marriage, a rewarding and responsible career, a beautiful home, and two delightful children, a son of eight and a daughter of eleven. Seven years ago her world was shattered, and a crack appeared in the fabric of her life that will never be healed. Her daughter was kidnapped, raped, and murdered. For an agonizing eternity of four days, Alison was missing. Her killer has never been found, in spite of nationwide searches. The city of Toronto mourned along with the family. It was a private and a communal tragedy. When a campaign to have the death penalty restored was mounted, perhaps its sponsors might have thought they could count on the support of my cousin. Instead, she campaigned against it and was an influential factor in its defeat. She also began a movement called 'Stay Safe, Stay Alert', concerned with child safety. She has appeared on television and film as a voice of sanity and care for others amid mounting social violence. She has made mercy transformative in a very special way.

I don't imagine that she often thinks of her child's killer with feelings other than outrage, anger, and grief. And she is entitled to her feelings. But she has not lived out of them in a destructive and damaging way. The crack cannot be papered over, healed, or denied, but out of that very broken place has come a flowering of mercy, and the fruits of compassion, care, and responsiveness. The broken place has been transformed into the source of new life. Mercy acts to transform.

And it is mutual. We all are givers and receivers of its gifts. I shall end with one final, gentle story.

❧·❧

In the parish where I live in Glasgow, I met two lovely elderly women, both well into their seventies. Both had had lives full of service, one as a teacher, one as a nurse. One had been married and was now a widow, the other had remained single. Now they lived together, and shared these latter days of their lives in quiet enjoyment of the small things of life. One of them was physically disabled, wheelchair-bound, and immobilized. The other could not talk as the result of illness. As the speaking one explained to me with great humour, 'I'm her voice, and she's my legs.'

In a spirit of mercy, compassion, and solidarity, they had embraced and transformed the physical limitations of their bodies and, in so doing, found the ability to affirm friendship, to offer hospitality, and to celebrate life. There was, of course, a hidden cost of suffering and courage implicit in their relationship, as there always is in mercy. But it did not have the last word. Humour and grace and generosity and care, these things had the last word, and they were contagious to those who came in contact with them.

Such a beloved thing, mercy.

6

THE CRACK

Blessed Are the Pure in Heart:
They Will See God

❧❦·❧❦

Linda is part of a big family. She has a mother and father, and several brothers. But for her, being part of a big family has not meant what we usually imagine it to mean. It has not meant love, companionship, support, people to belong to. In the olden days, being an orphan meant that you were entirely alone. It meant either that your parents were dead—through illness, childbirth, poverty, or war—or that they had abandoned you and their whereabouts were unknown. But Linda is an orphan who knows the exact whereabouts of every member of her family.

When she was three years old, Linda was taken into care. Such actions are complex in their formulation, and their wisdom can be endlessly debated. But such debates were academic to a little girl of three years old, started on a career of homes and placements, move after move, without security, without unconditional love, knowing always that her parents were not dead, were not unknown, lived only a few miles up the road. Over the next thirteen years, she became institutionalized. She lived in a number of homes in the care of many different people. Some of them were well-meaning, kind, caring, wise. She loved them, but they were not hers. Some of them were young and inexperienced, did not know what it meant to bring up children, and raised expectations in her that could not be fulfilled. Some did not cope very well with her at all. Residential care of children has never been adequately funded, its staff never sufficiently supported with training and supervision. It is a system that, as we are now all too painfully aware, is vulnerable to abuse.

Life in care was a minefield of potential hazards. Linda was a pretty child, and her sexuality was awakened at an indecently early age. Thereafter it was a source both of shame and of something approximating to human affection. Even if she chose, as she sometimes did, others would not allow her to leave it untouched. And she had learned that she had something that was of value to others.

As well as being beautiful, she was also bright and artistic. But her environment was not a good one for allowing her to develop her talent and to learn the self-discipline necessary for it to flower. At sixteen, she left school. At seventeen, she had to leave the home she was living in—it was only a home for those between the ages of twelve and seventeen. After some moving around, she got her own council house in a nearby housing scheme.

By this time, she was pregnant for the first time. The father of the baby was someone she did not love, and he certainly had no intention of marrying her. She had been going to classes at a nearby college, but had to give them up at this point. She could have had an abortion, but she had recently become a member of the Catholic Church and such a thing was out of the question. She approached the birth of that baby with fear and fascination. There was fear to be seen in the lovely eighteen-year-old who wanted to live life and have fun, who didn't want to go to discos with a thickening waist and hear the whispered comments. There was fascination for the unloved, unwanted child in her; a baby meant someone to love, someone to be loved by.

When the baby was born, it was a little girl. Although a little disappointed, because she had always wanted a boy (perhaps she felt boys were less likely to be rejected), she welcomed the baby and named it after herself. By this time, there were a great many people giving Linda advice, most of it conflicting—keep the baby, don't keep the baby, have her adopted, don't have her adopted. In the end, though, all those who gave advice, even the most caring ones, were not responsible for her or for the baby, week by week, day by day, hour by hour. They were not there when someone was most needed—in the middle of the night. Linda kept the baby, and for eleven months she struggled to be a mother. But it was an unequal struggle. She didn't have enough money and wasn't good at managing it. Life in care had not provided a sufficient framework for coping on what was inadequate to begin with. She was very young and pulled by many conflicting needs. But most of all, she had no model for mothering or parenthood, nothing she could fall back on instinctively. In the end, it all got too much for her, and finally, agonizingly, she gave the baby up for adoption, so completing the pattern that had begun fifteen years before.

Since that time, she has had three more children, with different fathers. And she has kept them all, and continues to struggle with motherhood, with relationships, with the daily challenges of life. Her beauty has lost some of its freshness, but she has never given up on the possibility of loving and being loved.

❖❖·❖❖

I remember Jean from my childhood. She was one of the stalwart members of the church in the place where I grew up, a new housing scheme in Edinburgh. I suppose she was what people mean when they talk about someone as 'a pillar of the Kirk'. She must have been still a young woman when she was widowed and left with three daughters to bring up on her own. They lived in a small council house and she worked as a domestic in the local hospital, eventually becoming the head domestic. I remember her mostly through the church, because that's where I used to meet her. Being a church that trusted its laypeople, and encouraged them to participate and believe in their gifts, she would often take part in the leadership of worship. I can still remember her simple, heartfelt, and beautiful prayers; not the actual words now, but the spirit behind them. She became an elder in the church and took on the task with commitment and warmth, coupled with the ability to get herself out of the way and be open and sympathetic to those under her care. She brought the same commitment and warmth to her role as President of the Woman's Guild, and her concern for people in trouble informed both these roles.

I also remember her as a very funny person, with an ability to laugh at herself, to stand up and poke fun at herself. Being a big woman with short-cropped hair, she was often called upon to play men's roles in the wonderful concerts the Woman's Guild put on every year, and she did it with great gusto and humour. And I remember that she was always encouraging, interested in what people were doing, always affirming their accomplishments, respectful of their difficulties. But most of all, I remember that she conveyed an irrepressible sense of delight and adventure in life. I remember one conversation with her, just as she was about to retire after a long hard-working life, when I asked what she was going to do with her retirement. With a gleam in her eye, this elderly woman, who suffered from severe arthritis replied, 'I'm going to take up youth hostelling.'

As a child, I could not have put a name to what

it was about Jean that was so attractive. Now I might say, and have had it confirmed by others, that she has qualities of humility, warmth, candidness, transparency, openness—a whole lot of words that have somehow to do with clarity, consistency, eagerness, wisdom, with putting herself wholeheartedly into everything. Today I could say that I recognized purity of heart. But then, as a child, I did not have words for these things. I simply understood, with a child's intuition and instinct for getting to the heart of a thing, that here was someone who was sound, who rang true, just as a crystal glass rings true when its edge is struck with a spoon. She was a big woman in every way, one with a shining spirit.

KNOWING IN YOUR HEART

It's worth exploring a little that recognition by Jesus of the blessedness of those who were pure in heart. Purity of heart is so often used as a kind of shorthand for not thinking dirty thoughts or having bodily desires. I think that this is to reduce the marks of purity of heart so drastically as to render them quite inhuman, inaccessible to ordinary folk, and there are no grounds in the Gospels for believing that Jesus wanted his followers to be angels, to reject their humanity—in fact, rather the reverse. He was short with those who 'tie on to people's backs loads that are heavy and hard to carry'. Similarly, the interpretation of purity of heart often heard as 'singlemindedness' has its own chilling, inhuman overtones. There are plenty of historical examples of singleminded people who thought they were doing the will of God, and whose intellectually driven scenarios brought death and destruction to untold numbers.

Perhaps one of the difficulties we have with this

statement is related to the changing nature and understandings of language. In our society, the heart has come to be almost inextricably associated with feelings, emotions; and the mind with thinking, reason, intellect. But in the ancient world the emphasis was somewhat different. The seat of emotion, feeling, was lower down, in the gut, the stomach, the bowels. There is a certain biological sense about this. Physically, these places are where fear, anger, sexual desire, and tenderness are most strongly experienced. That there was still something of this understanding around until relatively recently is easily seen in the language of the seventeenth-century Authorized Version, which is much more comfortable than we are today in referring to the 'bowels of compassion', and a belly 'consumed with grief'. Perhaps, though, we do still have a hint of it in our own colloquial phrase about having a 'gut feeling'.

And in both the Old and New Testaments, the 'heart' carried a much wider range of meanings—encompassing will, reason and spirit, consciousness and personhood, the true self, the inner man or woman. It was the governing centre, the centre of things. It pointed to a kind of love that was much more than simply an emotion or a feeling (though it incorporated these), a love that was a choosing, a valuing, a knowing.

❧⚬❧

For six years I lived on the Inner Hebridean island of Iona, working as warden of the Abbey. The Abbey is a large, draughty, and very cold medieval restoration, which had for many years been inadequately and expensively heated by a conventional electrical heating system. Not only were the people cold and prone to creaking, but the building itself was suffering, exposed to eroding forces of salt, damp, and wind. It needed a constant low heat maintained throughout the year to protect the fabric. The Iona Cathedral Trustees therefore embarked upon an imaginative and environmentally sound scheme to install a heat exchange system, drawing on the natural, renewable resource of the warm Gulf Stream waters that flow through the Sound of Iona. At considerable cost over two years of inconvenience to the residents, and with all the benefits of the latest technology, the system was installed and we eagerly looked forward to reaping the benefits.

Ten years later, the system, though efficient when it worked, had hardly ever done so: staff had spent fruitless hours down by the sea unblocking the filters clogged with seaweed; thousands of pounds had been spent bringing up engineers and technicians to mend the heat pump for it to work for a few days. The experiment was eventually abandoned, with the system undergoing a modification back to a more conventional form, a less ecologically good one.

One evening, I was drinking whisky with an elderly and wise local crofter. We got on to talking about the heating system, and he laughed rather sardonically. 'You know,' he said, 'I knew all along that it wouldn't work. If they'd asked me, I could have told them about the tides, and how they're peculiar here, and about the problems we have with the electricity grid, and a whole lot of other things. But they never asked me.'

He had the kind of knowledge that would have made all the difference. It was the kind of knowledge that could never be gained from a book or a course or a plan, because it came from seventy years of watching the tides, of fishing and sailing the waters, of working the land. It was the knowledge that had names for every rock and cove, that had walked every inch of the coastline in every kind of weather, that knew storms and their moods as we know our children's moods. It was that kind of knowledge of which the Bible speaks when it says, 'and Adam knew his wife Eve', meaning he made love to her. It was the knowledge of participation, of engagement, of love. It was what we mean when we say, 'I know in my heart . . .'

The Senegalese philosopher, poet, and politician, Leopold Senghor, wrote in the 1960s:

> In contrast to the European, the African does not draw a line between himself and the object; he does not hold it at a distance, nor does he merely look at it and analyse it. After holding it at a distance, after scanning it without analysing it, he takes it vibrant in his hands, careful not to kill or fix it. He touches it, feels it, smells it. Subject and object are dialectically face to face in the very act of knowledge. It is a long caress in the night, an embrace of joined bodies, the act of love. I want you to feel me, says the voter to the politician whom he wants to know him well. I think, therefore I am, writes Descartes. The African could say, 'I feel, I dance the other', therefore I am. To dance is to discover and recreate, especially when it is a dance of love. In any event, it is the best way to know.

So the 'heart' in the Bible was not just about feeling, or simply thoughts; it meant a way of knowing that comes from loving, a way of loving that is the difference between *knowing about* someone or something, and really *knowing* them.

The knowledge of the heart is a special kind of *seeing*. It is a seeing in which the other person is suddenly revealed to us in a new way, as completely and distinctly and utterly other, different, not-us, in all their essence and glory, infinitely precious, infinitely valuable, and yet, mysteriously, not separated from us, somehow intimately related to us. We 'dance the other'. The other becomes, in Buber's phrase, not 'you', far less 'it'. The other becomes 'thou'. 'Thou' is the language of the heart-knowledge.

John V. Taylor, in his great book *The Go-Between God*, calls these seeings 'annunciations'. He describes them thus:

> There are actually two stages in my experience. First, I am forced to recognize the real *otherness* of what I am looking at; it does not depend on my seeing or responding; it exists without me. And, second, there is a *communication* between us which I am bound to admit, has not entirely originated in myself.

Into this 'dancing the other', we are drawn, enticed, invited by the Holy Spirit.

Perhaps the most striking example of this 'seeing' in the Gospels is the story of the Transfiguration, where Peter, James, and John suddenly saw Jesus in a new way, a description transplendent with metaphors of glory, shining, dazzling, brightness. It was as if they saw what his within-ness, his interiority, was like, in a visible, embodied form. But it's not the only example. Jesus saw people in this way all the time, in their actuality and their potentiality, in their pain and their promise, in what they were and what they could be. And he responded to that seeing, that knowledge of them, with care and challenge and compassion, in an engagement, an encounter, a meeting in which, however briefly, *they were seen.*

'You never saw me.' 'I didn't really know him at all!' These are very sad words, and underlying them is a yearning, a deep desire to be seen as we are, to be known for all that is precious and vulnerable and tender in us, to be loved as we really are—not because we meet someone's needs, not because we are good, not because we play some role in another's life, but just because we are, and for who we are.

WHICH WAY TO JUMP?

They are profound words too, because they contain within them the implicit recognition of the brokenness of life; what I think of as the crack. 'You never saw me' implies the desire to be seen. 'I didn't really know him at all' suggests the yearning to have known. Always in our lives, we live with the tension between what might have been, what could be, and what actually is. And the tension is most acutely felt in our experience of the apparent polarities, the opposites in life. We are always being torn, buffeted, tossed about: between the desire for individuality, personal fulfilment, and self-expression, and the desire for union, communion, community, and belonging; between the demands and joys of the present moment and the thirst for that which is eternal, transcendent; between the need for security and the longing for freedom; between the urge towards spontaneity and the urge towards careful choosing; between wanting to do the right thing and wanting to kick over the traces; between the need for action and the need for reflection; between stillness and activity, silence and speech, giving and receiving, between being the centre of things and being on the edge of things.

These opposites, these polarities, these contradictions, are not in themselves the tension. They are not moral opposites; it is not that one side is good and one evil, one side is right and the other side is wrong. They are ontological opposites; that is to say, they belong to the nature of life itself. Contemporary physics has discovered universal energy under matter, waves, and radiations, a ceaseless movement of opposites, of attraction and repulsion, of union and separation, of positive and negative, from the smallest particle to the greatest mass. We are not different. We participate in this cosmic dance. The tension comes in how we live in the middle, how we take part in the dance. At every moment, the choices we make have the potential for creativity, for energy, for the birth of that which is entirely new, for life. Or they have the potential for atrophy, for running down, for stagnation, waste, death. And every moment, baldly put, we have to decide which way to jump. The crack comes when we realize that we have made the wrong choices! We see, with an often sickening recognition, that they brought stagnation and death rather than creation and life. And the crack widens even further when we realize that perhaps we could have done nothing else, or that it wasn't just our choices, but the interaction of our choices with those of another, that made them wrong. All of us have had moments like that, when we realize we've done the wrong thing, even though it may have been for the right reasons; or that doing the apparently right thing had in fact the worst effect. It is a feeling that combines an awful awareness both of power and of powerlessness, the power of the effects of our choices, the powerlessness of our inability to have the effects of our choosing.

St Paul wrote a lot about this inner conflict of existence, especially in the Letter to the Romans. 'I do not understand what I do; for I don't do what I would like to do, but instead I do what I hate ... for, even though the desire to do good is in me, I am not able to do it. I don't do the good that I want to do; instead, I do the evil that I don't want to do.' And he goes on to suggest that this is not a question of ethics or morality, of moral choices, because even when we do desire to do the right thing, we can't. And, far from being something that is simply a question of willpower (or lack of it) or bad judgement,

110

this flaw, this crack, is an existential reality; it is in the nature of life, just as a geological faultline is in the nature of life. He gives the crack the title of 'sin', meaning, 'missing the mark'. This sin has been so overlaid with moral overtones, with value judgements, that we have come to think of it as meaning bad deeds, naughty thoughts, nasty words. But these are not sin; these are the consequences of sin, just as the falling away of the earth, the landslide, and the destructive tremors are the consequences of the geological faultline. To say that sin is my fault is a different thing from saying I am to blame for it. The first is a statement of the way life is; the second is a moral judgement.

With the knowledge of the crack comes terrible pain: the pain that others feel as the result of our choices; the pain that we feel at having hurt them. They feel angry, betrayed, disappointed, rejected, unseen. We feel guilty, ashamed, humiliated, regretful, anguished. Both we and they live with the knowledge of injustice: we, because it seems unfair that we have hurt them when we did not mean or want to; they, because, whatever our intentions, they are still hurt. It is the point when good intentions really do feel like the road to hell, and hell is what lies at the bottom of the crack. And the crack is perceived at every level of existence—in our world, in our society, in our personal relationships, and in our hearts.

Of course, we don't operate with this kind of awareness all the time, or even very much of the time. We don't think of ourselves as making significant decisions all the time, of consciously choosing to jump one way or another. We just do it. It just seems natural, it's the way we do things, the way we learned things, the way life is. But sometimes, every now and again, something happens that is so shocking, so catastrophic, so extreme, that it jolts us right out of what is habitual, makes us look at life anew, shows up the faultline starkly. The experience of death or severe illness can have this effect, or the break-up of a marriage or other long-term relationship. War or redundancy can do it, or a particularly severe betrayal or assault. And there are some people, perhaps particularly intuitive or sensitive, who seem to have a profound sense of the crack, the brokenness of life.

※ · ※

DANCING THE OTHER

When he was a baby, one of my children would never eat a broken biscuit, even when it was pointed out to him that it tasted exactly the same as a whole one. As he got a bit older, we noticed other things about him. If something got broken, a plate or a glass, a toy or a tool, he would become very distressed, would sob inconsolably, especially if he had broken it, but also if someone else had. We realized that this was nothing to do with fear of punishment—if he *had* broken it, his remorse was always patent—or with the loss of whatever it was from his possession. It was simply that he suffered real pain when that which had been whole was broken. Now, at the age of eleven, that instinct for what is whole, true, sound—though still capable of causing him distress at the sound of breaking glass—has translated into an instinct for what is whole and true and sound in human relationships: into a keen sense of justice and fairness, an inability to tell a lie and believe it himself (he can of course tell lies, but he always knows that's what he's doing, which makes it hard for him to sustain dishonesty), and an urge to reconcile opposites, to right grievances, to heal that which is broken. From a very early age, he has seen the crack, has been aware of the brokenness of life. Perhaps all of us begin with this instinct for what is whole and sound and true, and only lose it when it is denied us,

112

or numbed in us, or allowed to wither away in us. I know that sometimes, as his mother, this combination in him of instinct for wholeness and clearsighted logic both humbles me and disquiets me, and then I fear he will not have a quiet life, will always be pulled to the edge of the crack. But mostly I am grateful for it, because it is a gift as well as a burden.

❧ · ☙

The first time we see the crack, the first time we experience the brokenness of life (and we all see it at least once), the pain is so great that our instinct is usually to try and make it go away. And we do that in a lot of different ways. We can try and make it go away by dumping it on someone else, in anger or misery. Sometimes we don't just dump it on them, but we aim it at them with all the force of a projectile, and all the capacity for wounding of a blast from a machine-gun. Or we can pretend that it doesn't really hurt, that it's not painful—act as if we are made of steel, put on a stiff upper lip, a coat of emotional armour. And other people will often encourage us in this, because they don't like to see our pain either; it reminds them of their own too much—as with this boy, described in Jane Millard's *Fragments of the Watch*:

'There, there. You mustn't cry,' said the woman to the child.
'You are the man of the house now.'
The child slips his hand out of mine. He stares mutely at the woman with fierce, brimming eyes, daring the tears to fall.
I know they will not. They will sink inward to the shattered, scarred wound from which she has wrenched and defiled his humanity.

113

But the cost of this kind of armouring is huge, both in the resulting emotional desensitization, so that we end up unable to feel anything at all, and because the pain does not thereby go away—it just gets locked up, like a ticking bomb that will one day explode.

Or we seek escape from the pain in any number of distractions—work, money, sexual release, drugs, drink, business, fantasy; the list is long, and includes religion. But the crack doesn't go away, and we have to do more and more of whatever it is we do to ward off its threat.

Or, because we vaguely recognize that the crack has something to do with the tension of making choices, of dealing with the opposites, we sometimes think we can avoid the crack by avoiding the choices. So we make one choice that we hope will spare us the necessity of making many choices. We jump one way and stick. We decide always to go our own way, we opt for self-interest. Or we decide to spend our lives always thinking about others, putting their needs first. We choose to live solely in the present moment and never to think about tomorrow, or we decide that we will devote ourselves to planning for a future that never comes, to living in a world of 'when my ship comes in ... when I get my new job ... when I finish doing up the house ... then I'll be able to re-lax'. We opt for the security of never taking *any* risks, always playing it safe, or we go for freedom, refuse to put down roots, shy away from commitment to anything or anyone.

All of these things that we do to get away from the pain of the crack we do because we feel threatened, because in some way our survival seems to be at stake. We are just trying to cope, and it's human to do that—an often unconscious strategy for what seems like an intolerable dilemma. We don't need judgement and condemnation for our strategies, we need understanding and compassion

114

and, above all, a way to turn the key that unlocks us from the prisons we put ourselves into with our strategies. Because ultimately our strategies have a way of becoming exactly that—a prison. The dance of life is a dance that embraces, requires, demands the polarities, the opposites, the contradictions. We dance when we are drawn to one another. We dance when we dissent from one another. But if we get stuck in union, or if we get stuck in dissent, if we get stuck in anger or we get stuck in guilt, or if we get to the stage when we no longer know what we feel, or whether we're on one side or the other, then we can no longer dance. We are denying part of what it means to be alive, we have become divided from part of our being. Instead of the creative relationship of union and separation, we experience a deep wounding and alienation. In our efforts to escape the pain of the crack, we make it ever wider and deeper.

And because this happens within our hearts, it is mirrored in our relationships and our society, and in turn is mirrored back to us. In the society we live in, there are forces that recognize this wound, this alienation, and that work to hold it. Into the crack, into the void, these forces leap, eager to help meet every need, numb every pain, create artificial needs out of the emptiness. We are invited to consume under the guise of buying back the very things that we lost when we stopped dancing. Because, of course, the *desire* for that which is lost is not itself lost. *It* is part of our being. It is simply denied or repressed. So if we have opted for self-interest and individualism, at the cost of communal joys and sorrows, we can pay to recreate temporary community with a group of strangers on an encounter weekend or to participate vicariously in the communal life of Greek peasants—though we may not know the names of our next-door neighbours. But the satisfactions of this consumption, the efficacy of retail therapy, is strictly limited.

We are hooked by the apparent offer of a large warm-hearted Italian extended family to buy our ready-made spaghetti sauce. But all we get is the spaghetti sauce. The market cannot protect us from the crack. It can only manipulate our alienated desires.

The drive to wholeness, to the integration of *all* the parts and tendencies and possibilities of our lives, requires us to embrace the contradictions of life, both in our relationships with others and in our own hearts. The Orkney poet Edwin Muir wrote, 'Time, teach us the art that breaks and heals the heart.' If we are to be whole, holy (which simply means whole, undivided), eventually we have to face the crack. We have to walk deliberately up to it, look into it, enter its darkness, knowing that in its depths are pain, fear, shame, impermanence, mortality. Or, for many of us, who find ourselves there not through choice but because we fell into it, it means staying with it, exploring it, bearing it, going through it.

THE JOURNEY OF THE HEART

I like very much the way that Matthew Fox, the American creation theologian, describes the journey of the heart. He outlines four paths that spiral in and out of one another in an ever-expanding journey. The first is the *Via Positiva*, the positive way, the path of blessing and beauty, of affirmation and thanksgiving for the gift and glory of all creation, all life. One of my favourite hymns speaks eloquently of the *Via Positiva*:

> For the beauty of the earth
> For the beauty of the skies
> For the love which from our birth
> Over and around us lies
> Christ our God, to thee we raise
> This our sacrifice of praise.

116

The Crack

For the beauty of each hour
Of the day and of the night
Hill and vale and tree and flower
Sun and moon and stars of light

For the joy of ear and eye
For the heart and mind's delight
For the mystic harmony
Linking sense to sound and sight

For the joy of human love
Brother, sister, parent, child
Friends on earth and friends above
For all gentle thoughts and mild

For each perfect gift of thine
To our race so freely given
Graces human and divine
Flowers of earth and buds of heaven
Christ our God, to thee we raise
This our sacrifice of praise.

(Folliott Sandford Pierpoint)

The *Via Positiva* is a spirituality of pleasure and delight in creation, of falling in love with life. It is the way we see most clearly in the wonder and discovery of young children, stretching their imaginations and intellect, exulting in their bodies, sharpening their senses, leaping to meet all the possibilities of life and growth.

But just as we come to birth and wholeness and light, so we also come inevitably to death and brokenness and darkness, to the crack. And we walk the *Via Negativa*, the negative way. We walk through the valley of the shadow of death. This is the way of letting pain be pain, of letting silence be silence, of letting nothingness be nothingness. Where there was gain, now there is loss, where there was fullness, now there is emptiness, where

117

there was height, now there are the depths. 'Out of the depths have I cried unto thee, O Lord.' Many of the psalms are the voice of those walking the *Via Negativa*. It is the way of embracing the shadow, of acknowledging our brokenness, our faultline, our sin, the wrong choices we made and their consequences.

It is stupid to deny the pain of the crack. It is the pain of bereavement, of failure, of humiliation, of rejection. It is often the pain of doubt, of despair, of fear. But at the bottom of the crack, in the deepest darkness, a strange thing happens. We discover, slowly and painfully, that the bottom, which felt endless, *is* there. Eventually we stop falling. We actually discover that it is holding us up or, like a dark sea we have fallen into, we are floating, and it is carrying us along. We suddenly find that there is the tiniest patch of solid ground under our feet. We take a tentative step—and the ground bears our weight. We begin to be able to see in the darkness—and our other senses sharpen. We hear more acutely. We begin to understand things we previously had not. In a curious way, we know the truth of words someone once said to me, 'sometimes, the darkest times are the richest'.

When we are confronted with the brokenness of life, our instinct is often to try to mend the rift, to paper over the crack, to do a job with sticking plaster. But we know that thereafter, there will always be a weakness there, that the bits never fit together properly again, that it will never work as well as before. What the *Via Negativa* and the cross invite us to is letting the brokenness be brokenness, because it is precisely there, at the bottom of the crack, at the deepest ground of our being, that new life is coming to birth, that resurrection is growing. 'Truly I tell you, unless a grain of wheat falls into the earth and dies, it remains a single grain, but if it dies, it bears much fruit.' We are invited to trust the crack.

For Christians, this process is embodied in Jesus Christ,

and represented every time communion is celebrated. In the broken bread and poured-out wine, we acknowledge the brokenness of life—the crack—and give thanks that in embracing this brokenness lies the promise of new life, life re-created, life broken, not to be stuck back together—but to be shared. Healing, wholeness, does not come in denying divisions, but by embracing them in a greater whole.

The gospel story does not end with the cross, and, in Matthew Fox's description, neither does our journeying end with the *Via Negativa*. Now we enter the *Via Creativa*, the creative way. We have been reborn into the dance of life. Out of the union of sorrow and joy, of darkness and light, of emptiness and fullness comes the power of birth itself. The urge to creativity, to expression of the new, comes upon us. We want our experience to bear fruit. Life itself wills us to bear fruit. And whether this fruit comes as parenthood or new relationships, as artistic expression or new areas of work, as a new skill acquired or a political engagement embraced, as a garden planted or a project undertaken, as the insights of our experience offered to others in friendship, counselling, or practical support, we are back dancing, generating new life, exploring new possibilities, new horizons, previously undiscovered parts of ourselves. We become transmitters of life.

In the creative process, on the *Via Creativa*, we are invited to play many roles. We may be virgin, opening ourselves to the movement of the creator spirit at ever deeper and more intimate places in our hearts and lives, to the conception of a new thing—a new idea, a new commitment, a new love, a new challenge.

We may be mother, allowing the new creation time for gestation, to wait, conscious and sensitive to the new life growing within us; then labouring mightily into the work of giving birth, co-operating with the life rippling within us and surging to be born.

119

We may be father, creating conditions for growth, conditions of security, comfort, care, steadfastness, the shoulder to lean on and the arm that steadies.

We may be midwife, encouraging, soothing, exhorting, reassuring, when the father worries and the mother grows weary and the child is slow in coming; who takes the strain when the moment is near, and draws the child triumphantly into life.

We may be child, coming to birth, pushing our way down the dark tunnel of the unknown, leaving the security of the past, the known, the familiar, to be born a new creation again and again, breaking the cord that binds us to a smaller, more restricted, life; making us free to live a new fullness of life. Not just one birth, but many births—or rather, the birth of new parts of us—the birth of new hope in us, the birth of new love in us, the birth of new compassion in us, the birth of new wonder in us. This is resurrection life.

But even the *Via Creativa* is not the end. Creativity of itself is a powerful force. But it also includes the power to destroy. The converse of creativity is not destruction, but stagnation, apathy. Creativity of itself is value-free, its energy encompasses the power to break down as well as the power to build up, to oppress as well as to liberate. The drive needs direction, the content needs form. The instinct to wholeness needs the concern for right relationship, the urge to freedom requires the decision for justice. We must choose not only *that* we create, but also the *purpose* of our creativity. And so we come to walk the *Via Transformativa*, the way of transformation.

The word 'transformation' literally means 'across forms'. It has a sense of something over or beyond, or on the other side of existing forms. To walk the *Via Transformativa* is to struggle to find new forms to hold our creativity, new ways to touch the heart. It is the challenge that faces artists of all kinds; it is the greatest single task facing politicians; it is the vocation of all who lead and enable worship for others; and the imperative for all people of goodwill who want to care in practical, enabling, respectful ways. The struggle for transformation is hard work, as known by anyone who has ever tried to write a poem, learn to play a musical instrument, or master a foreign language. It requires discipline, imagination, endurance, and self-sacrifice. It demands courage, the capacity to receive criticism and learn from one's mistakes, and the ability to live with failure. And of all the struggles for transformation in life, perhaps the most demanding is parenthood. After creativity, after birth, comes parenting. To nurture and cherish; to allow dependence and to encourage independence; to learn when to hold on and when to let go; to accept without condition, and yet to set parameters and guidelines; and to go on doing it for the rest of your life—these are the transformative tasks of parenthood, and they require all the qualities above, and more.

I began this chapter with the stories of two parents, apparently very different women. One might be called a successful parent, one a failed parent. But I do not see them as different. Both of them had, in their own way, the capacity to enjoy and affirm life. Both of them had confronted the crack, had walked the way of darkness, the way of the cross. Both of them had experienced the urge to creativity. What distinguished them was that one had been able to walk the *Via Transformativa*, the way of transformation, had been able to find the forms, the direction, the images, and ceremonies of meaning that allowed her to channel her creativity in positive ways. The other had all the right instincts, the profound motivations. But her own life had given her no adequate forms for parenting and, at least in her early parenting, she had neither the strength nor the imagination nor the opportunity to discover new forms.

121

In both of these women I saw the motivation to love and be loved. One knew how to do it, the other didn't. But both, in my eyes anyway, were blessed, the one because she helped me to see God by what was present in her, the other because she helped me to see God by what was absent in her. With one, I saw God because I knew that she saw me, in that I-Thou encounter. With the other, I saw God because she wanted to be seen, to be known with the knowledge of the heart. In both, I saw purity of heart, wholeheartedness, willing the one thing—in one of them actualized, in one of them potentially actualized. In both, I saw the struggle to love:

The Crack

There is a
   crack.
Jagged and
   long and
very deep.
   the crack
  is bleeding
having been torn
  a howl
comes from its
  heart
  how to get back
  together
with the proper fit
  in right
  relationship

the sides will not dovetail   neatly into place
  too much of the edges   having crumbled away
    nor can they   be forced together
without killing the fragile   flowers that cling to them
  the crack   is permanent
one must, however, stand   on either side
  as if it were not there   (although it is)
   (knowing it is)   within the good
loving the other   in its absence
whichever side it is   embracing it
  without that   crucial, agonizing coupling
    there is   only
the barren landscape of despair the blackened territory of
madness

    trust the crack
     it wants to be
  a wild, luxuriant valley
    with waterfalls
  a river running through it
    and on either side
  fertile   fruitful
     lands.

Kathy Galloway

7

COMMON GROUND

Blessed Are the Peacemakers:
They Shall Be Called Children
of God

My friend Marlene comes from Northern Ireland, but she
married a Scot and she's been living over here for a
long time now. Like all of us, she's shaped by the place
where she was born. Like many, perhaps most people
from Northern Ireland, that origin has a lot of pain in
the midst of the love. I remember that one time when
she was going to Northern Ireland to visit her family,
she became very anxious, and made me promise that if
anything happened to her and she should (for some irrational fear was moving her) die in the course of the visit,
I was to move heaven and earth to ensure that she
was not buried there, but see that she was returned to
Scotland for her funeral.

But that was a while ago, and perhaps her feelings about
Ireland have changed since then. Nevertheless, it struck
me as a measure of the kind of ambivalence, divided
feelings, that people from Northern Ireland often feel.
And why should they not, seeing that they come from
a country divided in so many ways? Marlene grew up in
Lisburn, a member of a staunchly Protestant family with
a strong religious faith—a gift that has been both blessing
and burden. Her girlhood was encompassed by the legalism
and conformity that marks so much of religious observance

and practice in both Protestant and Catholic, Loyalist and Nationalist communities there, and, as legalism and conformity always do, they left their mark first, in fears, and second, in the kind of doubt that inevitably presents itself to any thinking, honest person with the rigour to explore growth. The certainty and the absolutes that are characteristic of such strong religious cultures are based on clear and rigid boundaries beyond which it is unthinkable to move—'you shall not pass'—and that delineate a territory that must be defended (to the death if necessary) because upon it is security. 'No Surrender'.

Marlene trained as a teacher, and then, when studying to become a deaconess, she came to Scotland, as have many Northern Irish diaconate students. And married here, and settled, and the boundaries, which had already begun to blur and become more fluid, were firmly crossed, with the crossing of the sea boundary. In the years since that time, it is as if that channel crossing was the crossing of a Rubicon, from which there was no going back. She taught, had children, moved to Iona to become a member of the resident community in the Abbey, did some further study, lived her life of ordinary things: of jobs and family and hospitality and friendship. But always she has also been on an inner journey of moving beyond the boundaries and exploring the land that lies beyond—the land that lies between the borders. It has been a journey of examining and questioning all the certainties that she had grown up surrounded by in family and culture and Church, and of discovering which of these were genuinely true to experience and insight. It has been a journey of working for justice: in a long-standing involvement with Amnesty International, in volunteering in a peace and justice centre, in political engagement, and in a wide-ranging concern with justice issues. It has been a journey as part of the Church, and she, like many others who began firmly ensconced in the mainstream of a Church, now finds herself at its margins, where it sharply interfaces with all that is not Church (and, of course, the extremities are as much a part of the body as the trunk). But most of all, I see that it has been a journey of peacemaking.

A very great part of peacemaking is to do with 'breaking down the walls that divide us, and uniting us in a single body'. Another word for that is community. But that's not such a simple process, because real community is not the same thing as uniformity. Real community requires that within its membership, we remain different. This, of course, is a much more demanding thing than one whereby people simply think, speak, and act the same. Such uniformity is only possible where people sacrifice their personhood, and is not, in my view, real community. Real community is more costly than that. It involves a recognition of the ground whereon people stand, a refusal to invade that, an equal refusal to retreat to the safety of one's own safe ground, and a painstaking and sometimes painful negotiation of the common ground. And then it requires not being satisfied with that, but continuing to seek to extend and enlarge the common ground.

Marlene is a builder of the common ground. In her different living and working situations, I see her leaving her own, often painfully won, safe ground, going beyond the borders of that, inviting others to take the risk of doing the same, and working with them to make a genuinely common ground of the no-man's land/wasteland in the middle. It's not that you'd necessarily notice that that is what she's doing. The majority of peacemaking is not about building common ground between Serbs and Bosnians, between Arabs and Israelis. It's much more often about building common ground between neighbour and neighbour, between conservative and liberal, between man and woman, between parent and child, between one culture and another, between Protestant and Catholic:

between all the varied and subtle shades of difference that have the possibility to enrich us, but so often divide us in the lives that we live day by day.

For that task and calling, she has a number of important qualities—and I think that they are not unconnected with her own journey. They are, perhaps, where I see the blessing contained in her particular background. Because she has looked at the limitations, but also at the pride and the love of her own ground of origin, she is able to be tolerant of the limitations and the pride and the love of other people's ground. Because she has travelled beyond the borders of her own territory, and become in some ways an outsider to that, she is patient with people who are also moving, even if slowly, and encouraging of others who find themselves on the outside. Because she has known, and still knows, the pain of the journey towards freedom (and I cannot see that it has been in any way easy), she is immensely kind. And because she knows that she has herself been, or could have been, where others are, she has a great respect for persons. And (very importantly) she has the courage to speak her mind, and a sharp sense of humour with which to laugh at herself. Humour is one of the cornerstones of the common ground!

Most of her community-discovering has taken place in Scotland, but some of it has reflected her continuing concern with Ireland. Through the Corrymeela Community, which has been such an important seeker of the common ground in Northern Ireland, she came in contact and made friends with a Northern Irish Catholic woman. These two women, with a whole history of un-reconciled memories between their two backgrounds, made a commitment to one another. As a sign of the common ground *they* had found, they agreed that they would unite in an act of prayer. Brig would pray on a regular basis for the Protestant leader Ian Paisley. Marlene would pray for Gerry Adams of Sinn Fein. Furthermore, they would communicate this to these two men, and would write to them as and when it was appropriate. And so they did!

Of course, it is not possible to measure the value of this act on the basis of the effect it had on these men. What it did do was to demonstrate that there is a whole world of difference between uniting where you must and dividing where you can, and uniting where you can and dividing where you must. It was a demonstration of possibility—the possibility of common ground. This search for the common ground in all the relationships of our lives also mirrors the search for the common ground among the inner divisions of our own lives. Perhaps maturity is in recognizing the conflicts and splits and competing claims within each one of us. And perhaps their resolution is of the same nature. Rowan Williams has said that repentance is turning towards our victim, and forgiveness is turning towards our oppressor—and we all have victim and oppressor within us too. It's the turning that counts in peacemaking, the turning, often against our inclinations, to face the common ground.

And it's in the turning, even if it's in apparently small things, like Marlene's prayer and letter-writing and involvement in her community, that the biggest steps in reconciliation are made. To begin to be reconciled—with her past, with her country, with her culture—has meant both a journey out beyond the borders, and then a turning to face that which had hurt her. And that's not easy. Turning to face the common ground, breaking down the walls that divide us, so often means that our bodies and our souls have to be the instruments for clearing the common ground, for breaking down the walls.

But without turning, there can be no real peace. It's a making!

128

❧❦·❦❧

CROSSING THE BORDERS

For most people, like Marlene, peacemaking—turning to face and find and inhabit the common ground—means going beyond the borders of history, culture, religion, personality. But for some it involves the crossing of geographical borders in a world where so much is defined by them.

Ron was a man who crossed a lot of borders. I first met Ron briefly through his wife Jean, a nurse who ran a foot clinic for homeless people in Community House in Glasgow. He was working as a psychiatrist, having originally trained and worked as a GP, and subsequently practised medicine in Africa. But I got to know him well through living with him as a fellow-member of the resident community in Iona Abbey. By that time Jean had died, and he himself was retired. But after an active and committed working life, he had no great desire for a quiet life doing the garden and playing with his grandchildren, though he loved doing both. Instead, he ventured into a new life of travel and service and seeking the common ground.

I can still see him so clearly—a tall, lean, rangy man, with receding white hair, gold-rimmed glasses, and a ready smile. Sometimes he sported a beard, and then he resembled a seasoned mountaineer, one of that breed of tough, outdoor characters who look as if they can walk for endless miles and see even further. And he was indeed extremely fit, well into his seventies, could walk for miles, dig a garden, dance an energetic eightsome reel. And he was indeed a seeing man, observant, perceptive, insightful. But he never made a big deal of his insights. Modest, unassuming, diffident, he was quite without pretension, and had a disarming habit of admitting to ignorance where another might have speculated fruitlessly. I remember one occasion when we were somewhat exercised by the possible state of mind of a guest who was acting extremely oddly. Assuming that such an experienced psychiatrist would immediately be able to diagnose the problem, I asked him what he thought was wrong. 'I haven't a clue,' he said, and beamed broadly. 'What do you think?'

It was a characteristic response for him. Possessed of the kind of delightful curiosity about life and people that most of us have shamed out of us when we're children, he asked questions far more than he answered them—and asked them in a way that made people feel that he really wanted to know, and that their answers were bound to be valuable. This curiosity, combined with a great ability to get himself out of the way, made him a very good listener, and his listening, and his skill in asking questions that helped people to find answers for themselves, drew the most unlikely people to him.

Of course, these are not unusual qualities in doctors, especially those who have functioned in a psychotherapeutic context. But Ron took these things out of the safe confines of clinics and churches into a whole variety of adventurous situations. In the dozen or so years between his retirement and his death, he took the kind of risks that most of us don't even contemplate in our youth. He spent two years living and working as a community member in Iona Abbey—a way of life that is at best full and demanding, and at its extremes can be physically and emotionally exhausting. He spent almost two years working in a hospice in the Galilee in Israel, mostly as a gardener, but turning his hand to everything from dishwashing to being a tour guide. Here, he became increasingly aware of the complex and conflictual relationship between Israelis and Palestinians, and of the claims of justice as the basis for peace in the Middle East. This became a concern that was to stay with him for the rest of his life, and he worked unceasingly to educate and inform himself about the issues, and to respond practically wherever he was able.

He spent some time living in a small, intensive thera-peutic community in the North of England, another situation of great demand. But perhaps his biggest adventure demanded that he cross many new borders. Well into his seventies, he was accepted to work as a volunteer doctor in Nicaragua at a time when the Contra war was at its height.

To cross continents and enter a radically different culture; to learn a new language, not just in its words but in its silences; to leave the safety zone and enter a war zone; to cross over from affluence to poverty—these are border crossings that most of us would turn back at. And there were inevitable frustrations. He found that the medical authorities wanted to make use of his psychotherapeutic skills, but the difficulties of doing that in a language that he was just learning were all but insurmountable. But he came back inspired by some of the vision of the Sandanista revolution, not blind to its flaws, and filled with love for the courage and spirit of the ordinary people he had met there, and who had shown him such hospitality.

He finally came to rest in Glasgow, sharing a house with a kindred spirit, a retired woman doctor who had lived with her minister husband for thirty years in a village in India. He gardened, cultivated little plants and many friendships, remained active in his concerns, was secretly enormously generous, and wrote letters of encouragement to people who didn't even realize that he had seen their struggles. He died when he had a heart attack driving his car, a quick death that involved no one else, and inconvenienced others hardly at all. And left a multitude of people across the world who remembered with deep affection and gratitude the common ground he had opened up for them.

He broke down such a lot of barriers in his own person. The barrier that says, 'Elderly people are like this, or this . . .'. The barrier that often exists between old and young. This was the man you could feel confident about leaving to look after your children when you went away for six weeks to the other side of the world (as actually happened), the man who destroyed all the stereotypes of the youthful volunteers in Iona and Tiberias. A man who deprofessionalized himself, removed the barriers that often exist with highly educated and experienced people, not by denying or decrying his skills, but by getting them out of the way, so that what you remembered about him was that he made very good bread and brought you his home-grown tomatoes.

As with all of us, his spirituality, his profound motivations, were not just a question of wanting to do good to or for others. Anyone claiming that, is someone who has little self-knowledge, and which of us wants to have to bear the burden of someone living their lives solely on our behalf. Our spirituality is much more about a struggle to reconcile the conflicting motivations, drives, desires, and hopes of our own lives and this struggle can be a point of destructiveness and damage, or it can be the seedbed for growth and creativity. Or the struggle can be refused altogether, with resulting stagnation. That struggle is full of apparent paradoxes and contradictions, wherein failure can be success, weakness can be strength, death can be the opening to resurrection. I guess that when Jesus recognized and affirmed the blessedness of people, he was sharing an intuition that when that struggle is engaged in the depth of the heart, then it cannot *but* show up in the exterior circumstances of our lives. What is within will out. And the raw material of our inner engagement will translate

132

into the ways we engage with the raw material of our everyday lives and relationships. The inside of the cup is not the outside of the cup. But it is the same cup.

So there was for me the recognition that a man who was in many ways very private and self-contained should choose a life of extreme openness and vulnerability; that having lived contentedly in a good community of marriage and family he should then seek many ways to recover and extend that community; that his ability to be calm and restful for other people went hand in hand with a kind of restlessness that was for me a mark of the resolution of inner conflict that gave him real authority. Being a peacemaker, seeking the common ground, contains one of the strangest paradoxes. To find peace, one must face the conflict, within and without. In life, as in music, the most perfect peace is that which is brought by the resolved discord. And so the tragedy as well as the tranquillity, the tensions as well as the co-operation, the limitations as well as the freedoms, the frustrations as well as the achievements, the disappointments as well as the delights, the pain as well as the pleasure, are all written into the music of life. They are part of the same concert. The word 'concert' means, literally, struggling together. And that struggle includes the dissonances, the notes that seem out of place. Peace, shalom, is not about unison. It's about harmony.

I think there was something of the gypsy soul about Ron.

᚛ᚁᚓ · ᚈᚓ᚜

'THE SMILING UNRAVELLING'

Harmony, yes. But harmony is not easy, though some people sing in it with ease. Like many people, I sometimes find it very difficult to live with complexity. So often, I am consumed with the desire for clarity, for order, for the decisive action, the straightforward directive, the final word. I want the moment of truth, when everything will be plain to everyone, and there will be no more need for argument. We so much want this prayer to be the one that makes the difference, that petition to be the one that gets the message through to those in authority. It's hard to live with what we see as the inability of others to understand the logic of our case, with their failure to see sense. I know I live with the hope, somewhere at the back of my mind, that some day there will be a dramatic gesture, a prophetic outpouring, a dynamic leadership, that will cut through the confusion, the fear, the tedium, and bring peace. But another part of me knows that life is not like that.

I have always loved the books of Robert Louis Stevenson. I love his *A Christmas Sermon*. Somewhere in that, he wrote:

> It may be argued again that dissatisfaction with our life's endeavour springs in some degree from dullness. We require higher tasks because we do not recognise the height of those we have. Trying to be kind and honest seems an affair too simple and too inconsequential for gentlemen of our heroic mould; we had rather set ourselves to something bold, arduous and conclusive; we had rather found a schism or suppress a heresy, cut off a hand or mortify an appetite. But the task before us, which is to co-endure with our existence, is rather one of microscopic fineness, and the heroism required is that of patience. There is no cutting of the Gordian knots of life; each must be smilingly unravelled.

'The smiling unravelling of the Gordian knot.' Another way of describing the task of peacemaking. For such a task—requiring such patience and the capacity to live with

134

what is unresolved, to 'learn to love the questions'—a spirituality for the long haul is required, what Martin Luther King described as 'keeping on keeping on'.

❧❦·❦❧

The person who has taught me more than anyone else about keeping on keeping on, and about turning to seek the common ground, is another member of the Iona Community. In Helen's life, the crossing of the borders are clearly and starkly etched, because they have been such dangerous and hostile borders. A history teacher in an exclusive girls' school in Glasgow sounds like an unlikely candidate for civil disobedience and non-violent direct action. She does not fit the stereotype of the subversive radical: her hair up, her polite, well-modulated tones, her love of climbing and gardening, her enjoyment of Scottish country dancing. She could be any well-read, middle-class Scotswoman living quietly in rural Perthshire.

But she's not. She has a burning passion for peace that has led her to the gates of nuclear bases and into prison, to the offices of NATO commanders and round tables with army generals, into the white heat of the Vietnam War, and the freezing chill of a hundred vigils, demonstrations, and marches. She has spoken to a thousand meetings, gone on television and into print, preached and prayed and kept silence. She has inspired and infuriated and challenged and been a thorn in the flesh to many, not least to the Iona Community. To the core of her being, she is a peacemaker.

She went to Vietnam as a volunteer to help, to do relief work. She ended up campaigning for the cessation of all work that simply facilitated the smooth running of the war machine. Face to face with all the reality, all the horror of modern warfare, in a war in which civilians suffered in a proportion never before seen, she came to question not just the justice of that particular war, but the justice of all war. She returned to Scotland, became a member of the Society of Friends, the Quakers, committed to peace-making in every part of life, and was appointed the Justice and Peace worker for the Iona Community.

She has campaigned for the removal and disarmament of nuclear weapons. She has worked for the ending of the arms trade. She has attacked the injustices of poverty and oppression that breed wars. She has trained people in non-violent action, and acted as a mediator in conflict resolution. She held hands with thirty thousand women to embrace the base at Greenham Common in the movement to have Cruise missiles removed from Britain, and has travelled widely to speak for peace. She has represented her church at great church councils and addressed ten people in rural halls. She has led seminars and organized conferences, and worked for several weeks each year on Iona, enabling young people, volunteers, parish groups, and folk of every shade of political and religious opinion to engage with the issues of peace and justice. And she has campaigned ceaselessly and consistently against the Trident programme in Britain. This last has caused her to spend hundreds of hours outside the naval base at Faslane on the Clyde, watching, waiting, speaking to military personnel, supporting the peace camp there and, on occasion, cutting through or climbing the fence there. She has tried to take the British government to court. She has been arrested, and she has been imprisoned.

All this is evidence of a profound motivation for peace. She is one among tens of thousands of dedicated peace activists. But what people remember about Helen is not just what she does, admirable though they may think it (and not all of them do). It is how she does it. Her life's passion is evidenced not just in her goals, but in the ways she seeks to achieve it. It is not so much that she seeks a consistency of ends and means (though she does). It's more that she has fully owned the maxim: there is no way to peace, for peace is the way.

And so her campaigning is not just anger against war and the death-dealing trade in weapons of destruction. It is love for life and the beauties of peace. She is passionate for peace because she is passionate for life. And her protests at the gates and fences are not so much gestures of dissent as efforts to reach across where the borders are most agonized and most threatening. And her meetings with generals are not so much to impose her point of view upon them as to turn and seek the common ground. And so she proceeds with respect, with reason, and with reverence, as if to say: even your ground is holy, not because I agree with it, but it is because it is where you are coming from. In common with Ron and with Marlene, she has learned to really listen, not just to the words but to the silences, and to respond with grace to the stories and journeys of others.

This makes her a somewhat disconcerting presence. Judges sentence her with regret and admiration. Policemen hail her as an old friend, having built up a relationship with her on many demonstrations. And nobody wants to send her to prison! Not because they admire her, or because they fear making a martyr of her, but because they can't be sure that she will not start a branch of CND in prison.

Helen's passion and commitment, however, is not the singleminded, simplistic dogmatism of the fanatic. She is not out to save the world or the church or the nation. She is not interested in telling other people how to live their lives, or in designing master plans for saving them from themselves. She recognizes and respects the freedom of others to make choices about their lives, and does not seek to control, to manipulate, to impose, or to dominate. What she has done is to assume responsibility for her own life and actions. Personal responsibility, however, takes

place within a whole web of relationship, and therefore
confronts us over and over again with complexity and
the necessity for choice. Helen is both rigorous and disciplined in her decision-making.

Living with complexity and choice as she does has its
cost, is not easy. Mostly our inclinations are to want *less*
of the burden of decision not more, greater certainty
not less, answers, resolutions, everything cut and dried.
I have seen Helen exhausted, ill, frustrated, furious, dis-
mayed, and occasionally cast down into deep despair. I
do not say these things lightly, as of an optimist who for
a time has lost heart but will soon bounce back. This is
a woman who has confronted the powers of evil face to
face, and is not flippant. Perhaps her greatest despair came
quite recently, when Trident finally came to the Clyde.
After so many years of campaigning for its cancellation,
it could not feel other than failure and the end of hope.
Dissenters gathered on the banks of the Clyde (including
the affinity group that has been the source of so much of
Helen's own support and encouragement). They prayed,
they kept silent, many of them wept. Helen herself, with
a number of others who had taken their resistance on
to the waters, was afloat in a canoe. Somehow escaping
the notice of the military personnel policing the demonstration, she paddled her tiny craft into the middle of the
river—right into the path of the oncoming Trident sub-
marine. And there she sat, exposed, vulnerable, facing
the concrete (or at least, metal) actualization of all that
she had resisted for so long. As she described it later, she
was immobilized in that place, unable to move. It was the
equivalent of the Chinese student who stood unarmed in
front of the tanks in Tiananmen Square.

Suddenly, two Marines in a fast craft were beside her.
They shouted to ask her what the F— she thought she
was doing there. 'I'm trying to stop Trident,' she shouted
back. They laid hold of her canoe, and started to pull it

out of the way. 'Are you arresting me?' she asked. 'We're saving your life,' they replied. She burst into tears, and began to sob. When the vessel had passed, they freed her canoe, and spun her into the wake, where she had to paddle furiously to stay afloat.

Later, reflecting on this searing experience, she said that she thought people considered her to be foolish and foolhardy, and part of her was inclined to agree with them. Indeed, it is possible to have many points of view about what she did, including outright condemnation. What do you say about someone whose affirmation of life is so strong that it leads her to confront the final border, that of her own death? Paradoxically, this courage and affirmation has been one of the reasons that Helen has been able to work in a constructive and respectful fashion with military personnel. Though absolutely opposed on strategic and political issues, she is able to discern that thread of courage and affirmation in *their* choices. Never has she demonized soldiers!

❦·❦

I understand the incarnation as showing that Christ did not come among the powerful and the privileged, that the Word of God spoke in an unexpected way, took human flesh in weakness and folly, small, unprotected, and ready to suffer for love. In Helen's action, the Word of God once again, for me, took flesh in weakness and folly and regardless of its efficacy in achieving its *goal*, demonstrated the *way* of Christ—small, unprotected, and ready to suffer for love.

It matters to me that the Word is not made flesh in perfect, sinless people. If it could only happen in that way, then there would be no hope for me. It matters to me that Helen's life too is engaged in its own inner conflicts, that, in her, strength and weakness, humour and gravity, fear and courage, pride and humility, hope and despair all contend, are all in ceaseless exchange. Because I know she is not perfect, because I also have been angry with her, disagreed with her, thought her judgement wrong, her actions matter all the more to me. Because they become a sign of possibility. They show me that it is indeed possible to love your enemies, to turn to face and seek and inhabit the common ground where it is most difficult, most threatening, most offensive.

＊＊・＊＊

RELATIONSHIPS SACRED
TO THE SPIRIT

It's one thing to preach about loving our enemies, to hold it as a theoretical standard. It's quite another to actually do it. If the truth be told, it's really a pretty offensive notion for most of us—all right in abstract when we read about it in the Bible or talk about it in church, but quite another thing when out beyond the covers of our Bibles or the walls of our churches. Quite another when it means Mrs So and So who did us a terrible injury, or Mr You Know His Name, whose every word and deed we find objectionable in every way, or that member of our family—that former loved one, who betrayed us and hurt us most because we trusted them most. Or that country whose actions we find threatening, alien, and hostile. Enemies have faces and names—they turn up in newspapers, on our doorsteps, and most of all in our thoughts and fears and angers. By definition, enemies are people who have offended us, or our family or group or nation, who have assaulted, assailed our boundaries, invaded and laid waste our territory. They are people who have power to hurt and harm us.

Perhaps the first thing necessary in order for us to even

contemplate loving these people, our enemies, is to be completely honest with ourselves and admit that we find the whole idea intellectually, morally, and emotionally abhorrent. In our heart of hearts, a very great part of us does not want to love our enemies. We want to be able to go on hating them, and we reckon that we have plenty of justification for doing so. They have really hurt us. The hurt is not imaginary, the threat is not illusion. Only when we've embraced this recognition can we also recognize that this is not something we can do in our own strength. We need help, support, encouragement for the part of us that genuinely does desire to find a creative response to threat, to turn and face the common ground. To affirm, with Jon Sobrino, that loving one's enemies does not mean that they cease to be our enemy (that is, potentially threatening, hostile, in fundamental disagreement with us). It does mean that they are not, on that account, excluded from our love.

The power of love that most of us have within us by nature is mostly strong enough to love our friends. Mostly, it's a pleasure to love them. And, if we work hard at it, the power of love in us can lead us to love our neighbours—to act with kindness and fairness and understanding to those around us, those we meet in the course of our days, those with whom we already have something in common. But the power of love within us, the instinct to love and care and forgive, is not—in my experience anyway—enough to love our enemies. The love required to act in love towards the enemy, to go on treating them as beloved human persons, to refrain from damning them, to seek to understand their viewpoint, to hold out the hand of friendship even when it is slapped down, to face the common ground when from the other side of the border is coming a hail of missiles—for that we need a power greater than our own.

For me, that means that I need the help of the Holy

Spirit, which is the power of the divine love and creativity made available to us in all the things of our lives.

And so perhaps it is that the second thing necessary for us to begin to love our enemies is to make of everything in life an opportunity for the creator and creative Spirit to work through us. This requires of us not just that we seek the gift of the Spirit in our formal times of personal and communal prayer, but that all the conversations of our inner lives, all the stirrings of our consciences, all the thoughts of our hearts, and all our inward mental struggles should be directed towards being open to the Spirit. We turn at every moment towards the Spirit, we make ourselves ready and waiting to receive its 'dart of longing love'. In other words, we look for the indwelling of the Spirit in our whole lives. Not just when we are thinking about religious things (which I have a tendency to find oppressive rather than liberating), not just when we are at prayer, not just when we are consciously trying to act for the good, but when we are thinking about what to cook for dinner, when we are engrossed in work or meeting, when we are aware of our bodies and their sensations, desires, pains, and longings. The Spirit, as Zen Buddhism suggests, comes in to 'ordinary mind'. Nearer to us than breathing does the Spirit seek to come. And then, the Spirit that goes between and among people, breaking down barriers, opening up new and hopeful possibilities, may accomplish in us what we cannot do by ourselves, that we love our enemies.

The Irish ecologist and theologian, Sean McDonagh, has written, 'The Holy Spirit is the principle of communion, binding all reality together. The Holy Spirit is the source of all unity. All attraction, all bonding, all intimacy and communion flows from the Holy Spirit. Each of these relationships is sacred to the Spirit.' It is the Holy Spirit that both pushes and pulls us towards the common ground, and moves among us upon it. We gladly recognize the movement of the Spirit in our attraction and intimacy and communion with those we love. But it is a movement that also has the power to turn us around to face our enemies!

And though the Spirit comes as gift and not by our exertion of will-power, we can nevertheless make preparations to receive it, so that when it comes we are ready. And perhaps this third necessity is the hardest of all. Though we may know no attraction, no stirrings of intimacy, no desire, we may practise acting as if we do, so that when the desire to love is born in us, the framework to support and nurture that love is waiting.

I want to make it clear here that I do not mean pretending to love our enemies. I do not mean acting falsely and dishonestly, saying one thing in public and doing another in private. I do not mean denying our anger, pain, and disagreement. I mean being disciplined with ourselves, and helping one another also to be so, in not speaking those words, dwelling on those thoughts, acting in those ways that reinforce our enmities, breed resentment, or fan the flames of wrath. If we cannot be loving yet, then we can still try to understand. If we cannot be merciful yet, we can still try to be just. Though we may not find the Spirit moving in our hearts, we need not tolerate the hump on our backs.

When a child is learning to play the piano, for months and even years, her fingers will not go naturally and lightly to the right notes. She must spend many dreary hours practising scales and exercises, and make many mistakes. But eventually, through practice, her fingers dance over the keys, and she progresses from uninspiring beginners' tunes to a wide range of beautiful music. Because she has practised acting at playing, eventually she really can play. Imperceptibly, what was a duty has become a delight.

To open ourselves to the Spirit of love and creativity, though the words have a nice sound, is a fearful thing.

143

This is a powerful Spirit, this Spirit of connectedness. It is a Holy Spirit; that is, it impels wholeness upon us, draws and drags out of us potentialities that we would rather not acknowledge, have tried to hide, did not know we had. And because potentialities can always be destructive as well as creative, the Spirit casts us headlong into conflict and struggle, both inward and outward, takes us close to borders, boundaries, edges, and sometimes over them. That's where the framework, the discipline, is so vital, as forms to help us ride the storm, ride the tiger. It is a Spirit that has taken Marlene and Ron and Helen and millions like them to places they didn't want to go.

But most of all, we should remember that it is a divine Spirit. In facing the common ground, in desiring to love our enemies, in recognizing that we have to call upon the creative Spirit of connectedness to help us, we are seeking to realize the image of God within us. Perhaps it is this whole process that Jesus is describing when he said, in another part of the Sermon on the Mount:

'You have heard it said, "Love your friends, hate your enemies." But now I tell you: love your enemies and pray for those who persecute you, so that you may become the children of your Father in heaven. For he makes his sun to shine on bad and good people alike, and gives rain to those who do good and to those who do evil. Why should God reward you if you love only the people who love you? Even the tax collectors do that! And if you speak only to your friends, have you done anything out of the ordinary? Even the pagans do that!' (Matt. 5.43–47 (GNB)).

Jesus said, 'Blessed are the peacemakers. God will call them his children.' The idiom lying behind this phrase implies more than simply the kind of relationship suggested by the universal Fatherhood of God. This is particular to peacemakers. It is identity with God, not just by being human and created, but by demonstrating something of the divine nature and characteristic. So peacemakers display a real family resemblance, we might say. Loving the enemy, seeking the common ground, embodying the love that makes the sun to shine on good and bad alike, that goes beyond what comes naturally, and crosses the borders into the place where everyone is loved. Peacemakers suggest the life of God.

For me, Marlene and Ron and Helen are not different. They have all crossed different borders, borders of history and culture, of geography and language, of personality and enmity. But though the outward journeys have been different, I would not say that their profound motivations, their spirituality, has been different, nor that one is harder, more admirable, than the others. In their search for the common ground, they have all shown God-likeness to me. It is not required of us that we be like Marlene or Ron or Helen. We have to be ourselves, and face our own particular boundaries and borders, seek the common ground that is the wasteground or battleground for each of us. What blesses me in all of them, and in many others, is that they show me both *that* God-likeness is possible in ordinary people, and *how* one may travel towards the common ground:

The spirit moved my sister to a prison cell.
She didn't want a bomb to blow the world to hell
She knows that love is meant for enemies as well
The Spirit is moving in her heart.

Kathy Galloway

8

IF I CAN'T SING . . .

Blessed Are Those Who Are Persecuted
For Righteousness' Sake:
The Kingdom of Heaven Belongs to Them

🙢🙠·🙢🙠

Slag! Bitch! Cunt! Wee whore!

Ugly words, ugly and disgusting. Listen to them again. Slag, bitch, cunt, whore. Ugly sound, ugly meaning. Did anyone ever say them to you? Did you ever hear anyone say them to somebody else? Perhaps in a pub or through a wall? Did you ever say them to anyone? Listen to them. They are among the cruellest words you may ever hear.

People said them to Rose all the time. She believed them, she thought they were true. She even used them to describe herself. She had heard them so often and for so long and from so many people that she knew they must be right.

She heard them from men first of all. Right from the time she was a tiny girl she heard them: slag, bitch, cunt, whore. But at that time, they weren't talking about her. They were talking about her mother, her aunt, her mother's friends. Sometimes they were just talking about any women, about all women. Of course, her mother and her aunt and her mother's friends weren't nice women. She knew that from very early as well. They went with different men, sometimes for money, sometimes, stupidly, for nothing except drink or excitement or because they couldn't be bothered not to. They didn't keep nice houses.

There were dirty dishes, dust, decaying food, fag ends in the fireplace. Their children were neglected and went to school unwashed and unawake. Sometimes they were affectionate and kind to their children, sometimes they screamed at them, hit them, and locked them out. Since Rose knew that her mother wasn't a nice woman, she supposed that the names were no more than her due. The men who called her mother names, however, had got so much into the way of it that they applied them with a perverse generosity to any or every woman at certain times.

The men began to say them to Rose when she was about twelve. They were very young men, probably about thirteen or fourteen. They called her names first of all because she didn't, and then because she did. And they called her names because they'd heard their fathers and their uncles and their brothers using the names, had grown up with it, and had no other real way to think about women. They called her bitch and tease before she did it, and when they were finished with her they called her cunt. After that, they called her slag and whore whenever they wanted her to do it.

The first time she did it, it was because she knew all about it from her mother, and because she was curious, and somehow knew she had no other option, and because she was pressured beyond belief, and had nothing in her to resist. But she also did it because she read teenage magazines about boy-meets-girl and she was romantic and wanted to believe it could happen to her, and that somewhere in all of it was a thing called love. For the first few times she believed in love and romance, but as she kept on getting disappointed she also got disillusioned, and it began to dawn on her that love and marriage and happy ever after and three-bedroomed semis do not often come the way of a prostitute's daughter with nothing much going for her in the very worst kind of Glasgow slum.

So she ended up doing it because she had got into the habit; it was her way of life now, the men expected it, and because she quite enjoyed actually doing it sometimes (or, at least, the anticipation—the event itself was usually a let-down). And because of all these things, and because it had always been her experience, she knew that the names applied to her. Especially because she enjoyed it. If you're a slag because you've been forced into it, or to feed your kids, or because you're a bit simple, that's bad, but at least you can plead extenuating circumstances: 'I did it because I had to.' But if you like it as well, then you really must be the lowest of the low.

Perhaps you think I'm exaggerating, that people like that, life like that, doesn't really exist, that it's not really that bad, and people aren't really that brutal. But I'm not. I met Rose when she was seventeen and visited her in her house (I hesitate to call it a home), and for some reason we were able to talk to one another. Sometimes people in churches are a little ignorant about the stark facts of other people's lives, about the squalor and shame and stuntedness of the kind of lives lived in our country. But people who live a little closer to the sharp edge—teachers, social workers, neighbours, Women's Aid workers—will know that I am not exaggerating, and that this, and worse, happens. Not long ago I travelled on a train somewhere in Scotland, and beside me was a family with a toddler and a baby of about six months. For two hours I listened to the adults in this family talk in this way, not just as a figure of speech but quite directly, to the toddler and to the baby. For two hours I listened, and hated myself for not saying something, and could not think of what I might say, and something in me died a little on that journey as I imagined how these children would grow up.

And sometimes it's posssible to imagine that this kind of persecution (for that is what I consider it to be) is a function of class; that such things do not happen in well-regulated, well-groomed, middle-class suburban neighbourhoods. But deep down, that's a cop-out. We know that abuse happens everywhere (and are now unable to think otherwise as a result of disclosures from the media).

We become familiar (and familiarity does not completely breed contempt or numbness) with the extreme and awful instances of physical and sexual abuse. We pay less attention, as a society, and as churches, to the emotional and psychological and spiritual abuse that goes on all around us. And as we become more sharply aware of the catastrophe in our midst (as we have suddenly in Britain, as a result of some starkly highlighted tragedies), debate rages furiously as to who is to blame for these tragedies. Some blame declining moral standards, the failure of the churches to speak out clearly in moral condemnation, parental laxity, the breakdown of the family, violence and sex on television, the whole range of issues relating to personal responsibility. Others blame poverty, unemployment, bad housing, the failure of governments to take these seriously, the destruction of communal values and care, the whole range of issues relating to social responsibility. Arguments rage, positions polarize, blame is projected all around (rarely assumed—what we condemn is *other people's* failure to be personally responsible), justifications abound. And in the battleground, the casualties go on mounting up as the war rages.

THE PERSONAL AND THE POLITICAL

Reality, as usual, is more complex than the arguments suggest. The individual and the society, the personal and the political, are inextricably linked in an interaction that permeates every facet of life. The organism has no existence separate from its environment; the environment is constituted by myriad organisms. The organism seeks

149

from its environment what it needs for its growth; the environment reflects the level of growth of its constituent organisms. The interrelationship is total; it is reality. Attempts or pretences at holding the two apart are illusion, falsehood, ultimately self-defeating. Any society will be healthy only to the extent to which the relationship between the individual and the society, between the personal and the political, between the organism and the environment, is *right relationship*.

Right relationship is another term for what is called 'righteousness' in the Bible. Sometimes the Hebrew words so translated in the Old Testament are also translated as 'justice', and this is perhaps the primary characteristic of righteousness. But it's not justice in a narrow legalistic definition. Though it includes the meaning of divine judgement, it clearly suggests a marked bias in favour of the poor and the wretched, tends towards compassion and generosity. There is simply no getting away from the fact that righteousness, as used in the context of the Old Testament, and as proclaimed by the prophets, means, first, justice firmly rooted in the establishment of equal rights for all, second, a distinct tendency in favour of the poor and dispossessed (a kind of positive discrimination), and third, the establishment of these as fundamental to the possibility of salvation or liberation.

In the New Testament, this righteousness is extended, through Jesus Christ, into an even wider liberation. Right relationships, rooted in justice, with the imbalance against the poor firmly redressed, encompassed with generosity, *are* characteristic of the divine nature. To live in right relationship is to live in God-life. The incarnation is *both* the embodiment of this divine nature, the God-life given human flesh, *and* the demonstration of how this God-life is made possible for ordinary people, whose experience is that of right relationship broken.

Jesus recognized, congratulated, affirmed those people

who are persecuted for the cause of right relationship. It's not hard for us to recognize some of these blessed people, historically and in our own time. Prisoners of conscience, locked up because they have taken a clear stand for freedom of expression, for civil rights, for liberty of religious or political belief. We have admired and been inspired by these in every part of the world, from Martin Luther King in the United States to Irina Ratushinskaya in Russia, to Nelson Mandela in South Africa. People who have been imprisoned, harassed, tortured, and even killed because they sought to help those in distress without regard to class, condition, or colour, or because they have chosen to share the lives and conditions of politically oppressed peoples. One immediately thinks of Sheila Cassidy, of Pauline Cutting, of tens of thousands of medical personnel, aid workers, journalists, teachers, religious. People who have attracted persecution because they have spoken, written, filmed, lectured against tyranny and in pursuit of truth. People who have simply struggled to survive, and live a human life with their families in conditions of extreme oppression, where their very existence is a threat that must be put down to those whose comfort and security rests on inequality and the destitution of others. There are many millions of such people in the world. I think of Yanira from El Salvador, a young woman abducted and brutally gang-raped (in the back of a van), with permanent damage to her health—not even in El Salvador itself, but by death squads in Los Angeles. I think of a Namibian woman I met, whose feet had been hacked off at the ankles simply because she happened to be in the wrong place at the wrong time. I think of U in Burma, a Christian minister I met in Iona. He spent a week in beautiful, peaceful Iona, and we talked a lot. Departing on the Saturday, he spoke his appreciation for the week, and said that from now on, for the rest of his life, Iona and the people he had met there would always

151

be a part of him, and he a part of us. He was returning to a situation of grave repression, one in which persecution was inevitable for anyone who was even remotely concerned with human dignity and wellbeing. Though he is not often in my conscious thoughts, I know that he, and the knowledge of his courage in embracing the cost of discipleship, travels with me in the depths of my heart wherever I go. Across continents, he and I are inextricably interconnected, we are part of one another's environment that shapes the organism that is each of us.

Such persecution is clear to us, we can recognize the blessedness, the being-in-the-right place, the desire for right relationship in them. We see that, in their diverse ways, they participate in God-life, they are in solidarity with the cause of righteousness. And in them, we can also see that the blessedness blesses *us*. From them, we receive the gift and the shape of the Kingdom of heaven, that realm, that commonwealth of right relationships. They share in revealing the new life that we shall inherit out of *their* flesh broken, *their* liberty bound, *their* thoughts locked away, *their* spirit feared, yet breaking loose uncontainable upon the world.

The people who stand out from the safety of anonymity and passivity do so in the clear knowledge that what they do is threatening, and therefore dangerous; is open to misinterpretation and the great possibility of failure. Some do it from strong religious or political conviction and faith. Some do it for love of their families or communities or land. Some do it because they can do nothing else and still remain human. Some do it because it is forced upon them. All of them, I believe, are profoundly motivated by a yearning for right relationship (which may only be known in an intuitive sense of where and how these are deeply broken and distorted), by a spirituality in which burning anger and passionate love, care for others and an almost intolerable frustration at almost intolerable personal diminishment, desperate hope and equally desperate fear, collide and conflict and embrace and engage in a death-defying struggle. The yearning for right relationship is also the same, not different, from the yearning for right relationship within ourselves. Out of this personal struggle, they seek expression, creative forms, new means for the realization of right relationships.

But this is a somewhat theoretical way of saying that I suspect that, mostly, people have no wonderful clear picture, have no great notion of themselves as being in any way different or special, and quite often are not self-consciously doing what God requires. They have no overarching plan of action, no scenario to commend. Rather, they are where they are because a series of little decisions has led them step by step and inexorably to a point where they have compelled the reaction of the fearful, the powerful, and the malevolent. They have responded to an immediate situation, a domestic injustice, and it has taken them from caring about the people round about them to caring about the people round about them on behalf of the whole world. It is from such people, who are no different than you and I, that we receive the Kingdom, because they are its uncoverers.

And we receive it from them not only as a future promise, but as a here and now reality. In their lives they embody the promise and the pattern of the Kingdom, in flashes, in intimations, in sightings.

So we receive it in humility, and sometimes in humiliation, because it is the case that we who have much are dependent on those who have little to reveal the Kingdom to us. What God requires (stunning thought) is required for our benefit and wellbeing.

We receive the usually offensive gift of truth—not as an abstract concept, but as the opening up to the intuitive feeling for what is right and whole and necessary.

We receive the gift of courage, which is kindled in us

by the sight of very ordinary people doing very extra-ordinary things.

These moments of revelation, of *seeing* God-likeness, of seeing the nature of the Kingdom, though they contain demand within them, are, in my experience, curiously enough always experienced as grace, as gift. I am struggling very hard here to avoid sounding pious, idealistic, or patronizing, or of seeking to make emotional capital out of the suffering of others. But I remember moments when, as if a curtain had been pulled back, I knew that I had seen God-life revealed, life as it has the potential to be, and been stilled into a mixture of reverence, humility, and gratitude. I remember the costly hospitality of a bare and battered house in a Palestinian refugee camp. I remember listening to prostitutes who serviced an American naval base in Okinawa describing the kind of community life that sustained and comforted them in the midst of shame and self-loathing. I remember the joyful pride of children from conditions of great poverty in Burkina Faso dancing the story of their lives. I remember the deep faith and commitment to the common ground of a group of township young people of different ethnic backgrounds from Soweto. And I remember people a lot nearer to home.

ASSAULT ON THE POOR

I think it's sometimes harder for us to see both the persecution and the blessedness of people on our own doorstep. There are a lot of folk in our country who suffer what I would call very real persecution. My dictionary defines 'persecution' as: 'to harass continually with malignant and injurious attack; to treat with cruelty and oppression'. Malignant and injurious attack does not always come in the form of political imprisonment or the denial of civil rights, though we have a tendency to understand it in this way. Nor are persecutors always jackbooted guards or military dictators. There are many, many people in our country who are subjected continually and consistently to malignant and injurious attack: physical, mental, emotional, sexual, spiritual. There are many who are treated with cruelty and oppression by those they live with, work with, coexist with in our society.

I told the story of Rose at the beginning of this chapter because it is for me a vivid example of this very persecution. Here is a girl who from earliest childhood has been subjected to a particularly malevolent form of psychological abuse striking at the very roots of personhood, at her own self-understanding and self-esteem in a virulent and damaging way. The whole context of her life has been one of poverty, ignorance, squalor, inconsistency of care, lack of opportunity, and hopelessness. In the interaction of organism and environment, the environment has not only failed to supply what she needed for growth and flowering, it has actually attacked her roots with a kind of poison that has radically weakened, stunted, and undermined her potential. And the organism that is Rose in turn can give back to the environment only what is in her to give—a wretched sense of self, a promiscuous and indiscriminate sexuality, very little ability to function usefully in her community, and a tendency to destructive and antisocial behaviour. In her short life, she has known little justice, less generosity, and no salvation. She is persecuted.

To say that, to tell the bare facts of her story, is not at all to say everything there is to say about Rose. It does not tell you about her quick friendliness that leaps out eagerly and tentatively to meet you, like a puppy that wants to play but still has a fear of being slapped down. It does not tell you about her sharp, self-deprecating sense of humour that flashes out, and just as quickly vanishes behind a dark cloud. It does not tell you about an intelligence that is hungry for nourishment it never receives.

155

And, most of all, it does not tell you about her deepest longings and hopes, about her tender feelings and hurts, about the pain and promise of her life. How could it, when they are now so deeply buried that she has almost lost the ability to connect with them herself. People do what they have to do in order to survive, and survival for Rose has meant a hardening, a denial, a splitting off of all the areas where she is most vulnerable to her persecutors.

Who knows what will happen to her. Perhaps she will become harder and harder, learn to be tough, thick-skinned, to fight back, to wound others as she has been wounded, become a persecutor herself. Or perhaps the unremitting hostility of her environment will defeat her, and she will become a beaten woman, self-hating, unresisting, passive, dead inside. Either way, it is not a hopeful scenario for the children she will almost undoubtedly have. Or perhaps she will seek a way out in drink or drugs, pills or suicide. Or perhaps, in spite of every indication to the contrary, something in her will manage to transcend the limitations of her situation; perhaps one person—a neighbour, a friend, a social worker, a lover, even—will be able to communicate a word of acceptance and worth that will give her the courage to go on, and to grow. Who knows.

There are a lot of people like Rose. There are women and children who have known nothing but abuse in various forms all their lives. There are gay men who live lives of fear, suspicion, duplicity, and lies because they are too scared of a hostile environment to be able to live out of the truth about themselves. There are old people imprisoned in tower blocks on threatening estates who go daily in terror of assault, injury, and shame, isolated in a society that appears to have no further use for them. There are families, badly housed and jobless, for whom every day is an unrelenting battle to eat, pay the bills, clothe the children, maintain some shreds of pride and self-respect, whose ability to set boundaries for their children is stretched to the uttermost by the fragility of everyday existence. There are black people, especially those isolated from their communities of origin, whose daily experience is of harassment, abuse, and fear.

I do not wish to suggest that everyone who belongs to these groups is persecuted; that would be patently absurd. Nor do I wish to reduce people's personhood to symbolic categories. But I do wish to say that it is the experience of many people in this country that the environment in which they must operate is unremittingly hostile, actively assaults them and makes the establishment of right relationship almost impossible. They do not receive justice, they do not receive generosity, the prospect for any kind of liberation, personal or political, seems remote. We should name this for what it is. It is persecution.

Of this kind of persecution, Rose is a victim. But who are her persecutors? The mother who neglected her, the father who deserted them, the boys who objectified her? Yes, and yes, and yes. What about the society that housed her badly, that has no work to offer her, that stigmatizes her neighbourhood? Yes to that too. The personal and the political interact all too often in a kind of demonic indifference that results in the creation of systemic perse-secution. And in that, we all participate.

Traditional religious language would describe that systemic persecution in which we participate, if not as individuals, as a society, as original sin. If I was using that language, I would agree. But it is a language that I am hesitant to use. I am hesitant, first, because it has allowed the brokenness and distortion of right relationship to be confined to the purely personal dimension too often, and has not communicated how that participates and shapes, and is shaped by, the political/social dimension. Wrong relationship within and among individuals creates wrong relationship in a society. Wrong relationship in a society creates wrong relationship within and among individuals. And I am hesitant, second, because the use of the religious term often reduces systemic persecution to a question of morality, of ethics, of legalism (this is what people ought to do!) rather than seeing it as a question of liberation (this is how people may be freed to be different!) Law, as we all know, simply will not do it for us. And I am hesitant finally because to use religious language has the power for so many people to remove wrong relationship, sin, out of the arena of real everyday life into some vague spiritual realm. As if spirituality were something other than the real lives we live every day. As if sin were something other than systemic persecution, distorted relationship, stunted growth, and murdered potential!

The nature of the wrong relationship between victim and oppressor is curiously indicative of how systemic persecution eats away at the whole fabric of life. One of the consistent findings of those who work with abusers, those who have abused partners, children, elderly people, vulnerable disabled people, is that, far from seeing themselves in the role of persecutor, they see *themselves* as being victims. 'It was her fault. She drove me to it.' This, of a woman who has been constantly beaten to the point of hospitalization. 'She made me do it. She led me on.' This, of a six-year-old child. 'She asked for it.' This, of a rape victim. We hear this, and it's almost incomprehensible to us. We see the unreality of it. It is as if the abuser has not taken on the fact of empowerment, the fact that in this situation he was in the position of strength. And perhaps he hasn't. Perhaps in his mind, he's not the large, powerful adult, but the victimized child he once was or felt himself to be. The first task of working with abusers is getting them to assume responsibility for their own actions, to understand where power *actually* lay in the abuse, to see who was *really* the grown-up and who the child, to feel the awfulness of being in the situation suggested by this quotation: 'When he hits, don't fight back. You'll make it worse. And don't, whatever you do, cower away. It'll make him feel guilty, so he'll hit you more.'

The abuse fills us with disgust, and we can't understand what's going on in the minds of its perpetrators. Nevertheless, we are sometimes prone to the same syndrome, in principle if not in degree. There aren't many of us who have not, at some time or another, been quick to blame our victim when caught out in some minor cruelty, some petty injustice, some trivial offence. 'It's his fault that *I* shouted and smashed the plate like that!' 'She forced me to lie to her.' We all want to be justified. It's about the hardest thing in the world to assume responsibility for our own actions. We seesaw backwards and forwards between blaming other people for what *we* (not somebody else) have done, and taking the blame for what *somebody else* (and not we) has done.

This is not to say that we can go through life never losing our tempers or telling a lie, or making mistakes, or getting it wrong quite often. We cannot carry the burden of perfection. It *is* to say that we need to name these things for what they are; as *our* anger, *our* lies, *our* mistakes, *our* wrongs. If we can't do that, cannot admit our faults, then there is no possibility of forgiveness and making peace and starting over. If we can't do that, the lines between reality and illusion begin to become dangerously blurred, and we inexorably settle into niggly little victim/persecutor patterns. And we run the grave risk of losing our capacity for discernment, for distinguishing between reality and illusion on an ever-greater scale, and finding that eventually there is almost nothing we cannot justify on the grounds of our victimization. Assuming responsibility for our own actions (which includes both recognizing our own failures and those of others) is very hard. But it is the only liberation from living in the wrong relationship of victim/persecutor power games, in whatever arena we

159

play these out. Religious language calls this painful and often humiliating process 'repentance'.

And, since the personal is also the political, we can see the same pattern at work in our society. I sometimes think we're a wonderful country for blaming the victim. This child has grown up in a hostile environment that has failed to give him the means for growth, and the framework for becoming responsible. Now he's thirteen and stealing cars. Assault him some more. Put him somewhere where he can be 'corrected' with a punitive regime! This sixteen-year-old has had the bad sense to live in a house where she is sexually harassed by one of the adults living in it. Make it as difficult as possible for her to get out of the situation by cutting off benefit from sixteen to eighteen-year-olds! Will she run away, go on the streets? Perhaps. Then she can be blamed for her way of life. Perhaps she'll get pregnant, and then she can be denounced by a government minister!

Or you have a frightening condition that will cause you to suffer great pain, and possibly to die a most difficult death? You must be further punished because you contracted the illness by making love with a person deemed inappropriate (I wonder what the response would be if everyone who ever made love 'inappropriately' contracted such a condition!) or through your addiction to only one of the many addictive substances in common use.

I could go on. I simply want to make the point that a great many of our social and economic policies and practices punish and hurt most those who are already punished and hurt most by the hostility of their environment—the poor, the vulnerable, the unemployed, the very young, and the very old. Meanwhile, the capacity to assume responsibility for failure is not marked among many of the most powerful and privileged. No one resigns any more. But the sense of threat felt by the comfortable and secure grows more and more evident. And the reaction grows ever more punitive. It's hard to take on the fact of one's own power, even when one is sitting with all the good cards.

Blaming the victim doesn't stop at the English Channel, though. It's structured into the relationship between the rich and poor of the world, between the North and South globally. Sometimes it doesn't pretend to be anything else than naked persecution. Like in Rio de Janeiro in Brazil, where homeless children living on the streets are routinely murdered by the police because they're bad for business. Sometimes it has nicer names, like national security interests, debt repayment, conditions that need to be met for structural readjustment, cash cropping. All of these things kill poor people.

INSISTING ON BEING REAL

And yet, in the midst of this web of systemic persecution in which we are all caught up, there is good news. There is gospel. There are people who refuse to be victims, even in the midst of appalling hostility and onslaught from their environment. People who not only assume responsibility for their own actions, but empower others to do the same. People who resist persecution. Describing the main character in his play *The Europeans*, the great English playwright Howard Barker says of her, 'She is at odds with a society that requires her to be a symbol. She insists upon being real.' Wherever people refuse to accept all that degrades, dehumanizes, reduces them, wherever people strive to live out of the truth of themselves, wherever people refuse stagnation, opt for wholeness, wherever people insist upon being real, there, the cause of righteousness, of right relationship, is taken up. Right relationship can only exist in the context of that struggle, can only flourish when the choice is made to step out of the victim/oppressor game.

Sandra did that. She was a woman I knew in Edinburgh, living in a terrible stair in one of Edinburgh's hidden ghettoes. She was the chairwoman of the local tenants' association, born and brought up in the area, and living there still with her husband and five children. She was young, in her early thirties, they had no money, and a lot of difficulties. Her life had left a lot of wounds on her. But she was passionate in her campaigning to get rid of damp houses. She worked tirelessly, pounded the streets, organized marches, wrote letters, spoke at public meetings. Action on dampness led her to become more deeply involved in local community issues and politics, going beyond housing into unemployment, care for the elderly and people with disability, and education. She got to be a thorn in the flesh of local politicians and bureaucrats, her campaigns started to be successful, and she became a real community leader. But along with the success came the harassment. Her house became a target. She bore the brunt of every trick of petty officialdom. She was threatened with having her children taken into care because they said she was neglecting them. Eventually, the strain of it all began to wear her down, to tell on her. Fear and vulnerability don't go away. She had a breakdown. One day, she killed herself.

Refusing to be a victim does not mean that the persecution goes away. If anything, it is likely to intensify. What do we do as persecutors if our victims refuse to be victims any more? If they resist? If they refuse our definition of them? It's confusing and threatening when that happens. More often than not, we simply turn up the heat. Or we are panicked into knee-jerk reaction. What often happens is that repression increases.

But just as fear is contagious, so is courage. And when someone has the courage to refuse to be a victim, other people are empowered to begin to do the same. And perhaps the contagion of courage where it was not

162

expected offers us an opportunity to look again at the power game and to see that it's not a good game, and that it damages us as the persecutor as well. And we choose, even just this once, not to play it with anyone else (because we can't play it with our original victim).

Scottish Women's Aid have produced what they call a Bill of Rights for Women. It was written for women who are in any way ill-treated or frightened by the men they live with. This is what it says:

I am not to blame for being beaten and abused.
I am not the cause of someone else's violent behaviour.
I do not like it or want it.
I do not have to take it.
I am an important human being.
I am a worthwhile woman.
I deserve to be treated with respect.
I do have power to take good care of myself.
I can decide for myself what is best for me.
I can make changes in my life if I want to.
I am not alone. I can ask others to help me.
I am worth working for and changing for.
I deserve to make my own life safe and happy.

It's worth reading through a few times. Is some of it difficult for us to read? There is a certain strand of Christian thought that has sometimes tried to make people think that they (perhaps especially women) are obliged as our Christian duty to put up with any and every kind of ill-treatment and injustice. This is codswallop. There is all the difference in the world between forgiving an injustice, and pretending it's not an injustice, between caring about other people and thinking that we don't matter, between turning to seek the common ground and permitting our own ground to be invaded, trampled down, and destroyed.

The message of the gospel is that we *all* matter. We are not invited to love other people instead of ourselves. We are invited to love them *as* we love ourselves. If we cannot love ourselves, the love we are able to give to others is at best fragmented.

If God-life, the Kingdom of heaven, is characterized by right relationship, by justice, generosity, and liberation (biblically, liberation is the root meaning 'salvation'—'the breaking into an open space which provides room for growth and development'), and if we are invited to live in accordance with that God-life, then acceptance of injustice, meanness, and bondage is to accept wrong relationship. The message of self-worth is not a substitute for care for others, by the same token. It is not a case of either/or. Self-worth is a prerequisite for right relationship with others.

The gospel message is that our worth, our value, our infinite preciousness, does not have to be earned, deserved, or won. It is gift. It is unconditional. It is in the nature of God that we are loved in this way.

And so for me the Bill of Rights for Women's Aid is gospel, good news. It is the word of unconditional value, the word that says: you do not have to be a victim. You can live as a free and responsible person. But if it's true for me, then it must also be true for everyone else. For men. For children. Perhaps it is even true for all the species and forms on earth (with whom we are also in relationship, and with whom it is perhaps important that we also be in right relationship). And, just as being a peacemaker inevitably leads to and through conflict and difference to the common ground, so being a responsible person also leads to and through conflict and difference to right relationship. Justice for you *and* justice for me. Generosity for you *and* generosity for me. Liberation for you *and* liberation for me. When we are not part of the victim/persecutor power games, when we are equally responsible, we have to find new ways of resolving issues, of balancing needs, of negotiating conflicts, of solving problems. This is a lifelong struggle, because we are never fully there, always on the way, can only notch up little accomplishments—within us and around us and among us.

But the intimations of God-life that are revealed to us especially by those who are persecuted for their revelations fire our courage, strengthen our endurance, liberate our imaginative possibilities. And what of them, who bless *us* by their intimations of the Kingdom? Are their blessings only to be in the mysterious life that transcends space and time? What of those who are in anguish in the present because they are persecuted for the cause of righteousness? What about those who hurt, and suffer hell? What about Sandra, who gave all that she had, including her own life in despair? All I am able to say is what I have found to be true to experience, my own, but mostly the experience of others: that this cross, this crucial place of struggle and suffering and conflict and love, leads somehow to resurrection life, life transformed, life in all its fullness—in a relationship restored to right relationship, in a thought suspended timeless for a moment, in a cry answered, a sense intensified, in delight in the midst of pain, in freedom unchained by persecution. In these resurrection moments, these moments of grace, I have a kind of sense that that is the real life that encompasses us all around, waiting to break through, and that Sandra has broken through to live in it, and that it belongs to her.

And so I am not inclined to beat my breast too much. I *am* inclined to remember her and give thanks. We don't suffer for our children, for our friends, for ourselves, in order that they, and we, should suffer more. We do it so that they, and we, may sing and dance. 'If I can't sing, I don't want your revolution.' (Rosa Luxemburg).

I can hear her saying that.

❦·❧

165